W9-AQM-695

Labor, Business, and Change in Germany and the United States

Kirsten S. Wever
Editor

2001

W.E. Upjohn Institute for Employment Research
Kalamazoo, Michigan

Library of Congress Cataloging-in-Publication Data

Labor, business, and change in Germany and the United States /
Kirsten S. Wever, editor.
    p. cm.
    Includes bibliographical references and index.
    ISBN 0–88099–216–6 (cloth : alk. paper) — ISBN 0–88099–215–8 (pbk. : alk.
paper)
        1. Industrial relations—Germany. 2. Industrial relations—United States.
    3. Telecommunication—Deregulation—Germany. 4. Telecommunication—
    Deregulation—United States. 5. Labor unions—Germany.
    6. Labor unions—United States. I. Wever, Kirsten S.

    HD8451 .L33 2001
    331'.0943—dc21

                                                                    2001026024

The facts presented in this study and the observations and viewpoints expressed are
the sole responsibility of the authors. They do not necessarily represent positions of
the W.E. Upjohn Institute for Employment Research.

Cover design by J.R. Underhill.
Index prepared by Nancy K. Humphreys.
Printed in the United States of America.

Contents

Preface

This volume is the result of a two-year German-American Project on Mutual Learning, organized by members of the Industrial Relations Section at the Sloan School of Management, Massachusetts Institute of Technology. The project was launched by Tom Kochan and Richard Locke, with help from Nicholas Ziegler and me. We benefited from cooperation and collaboration with Frieder Naschold and various other colleagues at the Science Center (Wissenschaftszentrum) in Berlin.

In two conferences, in Washington, D.C. in 1994 and Berlin in 1996, we brought together researchers in comparative industrial and employment relations and comparative political economy. The conferences yielded stimulating dialogue about the processes by which social actors in advanced capitalist economies might learn from each other. Some of the conference papers have been revised for this volume. Our aim was to encourage explicitly comparative debates and written work and to go beyond the intellectual and practical insights of research focused on single-country cases. We were interested in bringing to the surface and clarifying key analytical and policy insights, based on empirical research in a variety of political economic arenas in both countries. It was our goal that these insights would inform our understanding of how practitioners and policymakers in different countries might learn from each other.

The areas of comparison covered in this volume are far from exclusive. The constellation of arenas explored here results in part from design and in part from circumstance. Our initial aim was not to impose a set of issues for comparison, but rather to bring together scholars focusing on a range of issues related to employment relations. We believed these meetings would make clear which empirical areas were most germane to the strategic shifts and dislocations occurring in both countries today. To some extent, then, the content of this volume was determined by the subjects of interest to the scholars we brought together under the aegis of the German-American Project.

For this reason, this book does not cover, among other things, the different ways in which women and men experience employment relations dynamics and outcomes. In our effort to capitalize on the best available research in comparative political economy, we could find no natural selection criteria, and it was perhaps inevitable that important areas of political economic activity would be left out. It is our hope that the breadth and sweep made possible by our loose methodological approach will compensate for this weakness.

We are indebted to the German-American Academic Council Foundation for generous financial support for our project and to the German Marshall

Fund of the United States and the Center for European Studies at Harvard University, which also helped fund this work. The project's aims and the conferences are discussed fully in our proposal and in the interim and final reports (Kochan, Naschold, and Wever 1995, 1996; Kochan and Naschold 1994).

References

Kochan, Thomas, and Frieder Naschold. 1994. "Mutual Learning: The Transformation of German and American Labor Policies and Institutions." Proposal to the German-American Academic Council, Massachusetts Institute of Technology, Cambridge, Massachusetts.

Kochan, Thomas, Frieder Naschold, and Kirsten S. Wever. 1995. "Mutual Learning: The Transformation of German and American Labor Policies and Institutions." Interim report delivered to the German-American Academic Council, Washington D.C.

_____. 1996. "Final Report to the German-American Academic Council Foundation." Sloan School of Management, Industrial Relations Section, Massachusetts Institute of Technology, and Sloan School of Management and Labor Relations, Department of Labor Studies and Employment Relations, Rutgers University.

1

Mutual Learning with Trade-Offs

Kirsten Wever

Rutgers University

Comparative social scientists have never quite explained how economic and political practitioners and decision makers in different countries learn from each other. The question has gained policy relevance over the past two decades with the transformation of the assembly line and mass production, the rise of new service industries, and the globalization of most domestic economies. With Japan still recovering from its severest social and economic shock in the postwar period, it makes intuitive sense to shift our focus to the United States and Germany for cues. Both appear to be in better political economic shape than Japan in a variety of ways noted in this volume. Both countries have apparently intransigent and hardly insignificant shortcomings. Both because of and in spite of these problems, we believe than comparisons between the German and American models are especially illuminating.

The chapters in this book compare sectoral and firm-level adjustment processes, modes of innovation, and processes of change, focusing on examples of and possibilities for cross-border and cross-sectoral learning in Germany and the United States. In one way or another, each chapter also explores the proposition that the benefits of German coordinating institutions and of the United States' more decentralized political economy each entail trade-offs that may be necessary and are certainly politically unpleasant.

Cross-border and cross-sectoral learning are as difficult to understand as to undertake. Piecemeal learning is hampered by the interconnectedness of political economic systems, with changes on one dimension necessarily affecting, and affected by, others. At the same time, the wholesale transfer of institutional systems is unlikely in the absence of major political displacement caused by war and occupation. Yet a substantial and growing body of empirical evidence has led to a loose scholarly consensus that considerable transfer of some sort is occurring across national borders generally, and especially between Germany and the United States. Certainly it is not the case that practices identified in one setting, such as the German apprenticeship training system or different types of "lean production," are being quickly, easily, or completely lifted across national borders and copied. Instead, corporate actors, powerful individuals, policymakers, or policymaking bodies are engaged in iterative, experimental, and partial efforts at transferring and adapting certain concepts and practices. Institutional/organizational transfer takes a back seat to various dynamic, even volatile, processes of learning, compromise, adjustment, and innovation, usually among actors "on the ground" rather than in the context of national competitiveness policies. Therefore, what we can learn from previous work in this area is limited.

Indeed, much past research and theorizing in both countries has focused on how institutions can be transferred at the macro (national) level (Jacoby 1997). In the United States, such debates—for instance, about importing apprenticeship training institutions or works councils—have never gained a great deal of momentum, not least because of the obvious and numerous obstacles posed by the functioning of and relationship among U.S. banks, companies, workers, unions, and the environment in which they operate. In Germany, debates about the decentralization of industrial and employment relations and the deregulation of markets (including the labor markets) have continued to bump up against the strategic resistance of unions as well as large segments of the employer community, and more recently against the small but growing influence of the European Union's social policy agenda. Meanwhile, however, individual actors are busy establishing new operations, managing joint ventures and collective interests, developing labor–management innovations, and learning from each other's successes and failures.

A great deal has been written about the benefits to labor and business of Germany's coordinated institutionalized system of employment relations (see, e.g., Wever 1995; Turner 1991). Yet one important unanswered question for Germans is how to minimize the constraining aspects of this system while maximizing the supportive aspects of national and sectoral institutional frameworks. For instance, can industry-wide coordination of employment relations, which takes some of the costs of labor out of competition among employers, be combined with vigorous local innovations?

Germany's framework institutions have been famous for addressing market failures which individual local actors may not want or be able to address, but which ultimately detract from the common good. The training system is the most obvious case in point. Can local U.S. actors make the practical distinction between the problematic (time-consuming) and the beneficial (cost-sharing) aspects of Germany's framework institutions? Can the latter be supported in an environment that naturally bypasses or compensates for the former?

It is widely agreed that by international standards the Americans are especially good at rapidly developing and executing impressive innovations—from labor–management relations to the reorganization of production/service delivery or the training of managers—because of the diverse and decentralized nature of the country's political economy. Not surprisingly, Germans are examining which aspects of the decentralized U.S. system spur innovation. What is undoubtedly more complicated is disentangling these from the forces that can inhibit innovation, or its diffusion across settings, or the diffusion of its social and economic benefits. How much and what kind of institutional framework do we need to avoid these problems, and what will it cost whom? Recent pressures in Germany to rein in public spending and lower unemployment, deriving in part from the consolidation of the European Union's economic agenda, bring new urgency to this issue.

Finally, how much room is there for cross-sectoral learning, both among and within countries? Could innovations in interfirm cooperation in the German electronics sector and in more flexible employment relations (especially in the *Neue Länder*[1]) help map out how local actors might accommodate changes in what is negotiated, by whom, and how? Could companies in the United States develop loose framework institutions for joint training programs that could avoid "poaching,"[2] lessen pressures for head-to-head competition, and ultimately produce more highly skilled workforces? Could such framework institutions be structured so as to adapt themselves to changing external pressures, as suggested by Thelen (1991)?

INSTITUTIONS, IDEAS, AND
THE IMPETUS FOR LEARNING

Mutual learning takes place at the intersection of institutions, ideas or cultures, and actors' often competing strategies. Lessons reside in the great strengths and weaknesses of both countries in various political economic arenas. The authors of this volume share the view that significant mutual learning between the two countries will require careful consideration of the contexts that structure how actors think about and carry out the strategies they perceive to be available; of how actors can, at least in principle, change those institutions; and of what cross-national and subnational/cross-sectoral (or cross-case) comparisons imply about the malleability of institutions and actor strategies. Examining these areas has become increasingly important in recent years, because change, adjustment, and innovation—whether indigenous or transferred from abroad—have all taken on increasingly pressing relevance to political economies and therefore to policymakers and practitioners throughout the advanced capitalist countries.

Why should social actors in the United States and Germany be especially interested in learning from each other? Germany and the United States remain the two most powerful western economies and have over several decades been ranked the world's number one and two exporters. Germany's core economy remains sound, notwithstanding still-high unemployment in the east. Indeed, many of Germany's problems can be traced directly to the still-astronomical costs of unification. The United States economy remains fundamentally robust, despite the slowdown that began near the end of the year 2000, and its low unemployment levels are the envy of many advanced capitalist countries.

But the 1980s and 1990s have exposed cracks in the foundations of Germany's social market economy and of the more free market United States approach. Germany is experiencing far greater difficulties in integrating the eastern and western economies and societies than was anticipated at the time of unification in 1990. Official unemployment in eastern Germany remains well over the EU average (which is hovering between 8 and 12 percent), and social tensions have spawned politically disruptive and even frightening debates about underlying causes. Many employers insist the problems are chiefly related to high labor costs and centralized bargaining. Yet studies have found significant organizational and managerial rigidities, which surely play into the slow pace of change that contributes to Germany's competitiveness problems, especially in the service and high-technology sectors (Walgenbach 1993; Lane 1989). Similarly, it has become common to criticize the German economy for its lack of easily available venture capital and for various other innovation-inhibiting features of its financial system.

In the United States, macrolevel indicators of overall economic competitiveness have long been paralleled by extreme disparities in earnings and wealth. These disparities are starkly visible in certain regions, sectors, and subsectors, which remain extraordinarily underdeveloped by the standards of the advanced capitalist world. Inequality is perpetuated by and reflected in the fragmented nature of employment relations: well-paying union and nonunion jobs in strong manufacturing and service industries exist alongside extremely insecure, low-paying, mostly nonunion jobs in smaller, weaker companies and industries. Such inequalities would not arise in Germany because of the presence of strong, central coordinating institutions in the areas of employment relations and related aspects of the political economy. Closely linked to this patchwork quilt of work and employment in the United States is the extremely uneven quality of workers' and managers' skills, which has alarming implications for even medium-term national competitiveness.

Our focused comparisons of specific political economic domains in these two countries allows us to avoid what Hyman (1994, p. 1) calls "the crude juxtaposition of superficial and ill-digested data . . . or else a gauche imposition on national experience of preset taxonomies." These chapters report on original research by scholars who share a loose, institutional analytical approach and an interest in understanding work and employment relationships in their political economic contexts. We focus on four contemporary arenas of political economic change: telecommunications deregulation and privatization, management development systems, supplier relations, and employment relations.

Much comparison—especially of the United States and Germany—has had an implicit bias toward one or another model. In the 1970s, it was fashionable among social scientists to argue that social democratic institutions are good per se and that we should all learn from countries like Germany. In fact, of course, institutions will always constrain some actors while supporting others, and precisely which actors are constrained or supported changes over time. For example, in the 1930s and early 1940s, the United States employer community saw itself as benefiting from the Wagner Act, which governed union–management relations in most sectors. This act appeared to guarantee labor peace and far-ranging managerial prerogatives. Today, most employers and even some unionists are actively hostile to that legal framework. In 1952, German unions and employers were extremely anxious about the effects of the Works Constitution Act which regulated codetermination at the workplace by instituting the most powerful works councils in Europe. Currently, many German employers are positively inclined toward the councils and most unions see them as powerful allies at the point of production. In short, institutions per se are not good or bad, but the functions they perform for society and the economy at a given point in time certainly can be (see, for example, Dore 1973; Maurice, Sellier, and Sylvestre 1986; see also Berger and Piore 1980).

The idea of "best institutions" has its analog in that of "best practice," according to which firm-level flexibility is good in and of itself, and which implies that everyone should learn from the United States. Throughout the 1980s, the business press promoted certain corporate practices as more or less context-independent solutions to common international pressures (see, for instance, Hamel and Prahalad 1994; Kotter and Heskett 1992; Womack, Jones, and Roos 1991). Since the collapse of the Soviet system, business consultants and scholars have broadened their prescriptions to encompass "best" economic institutions as well (Naisbitt 1997; Porter 1998). In greater or lesser measure, these works are premised on the notion that there are single best ways for corporations to organize work, production, and service delivery and, at least by implication, for societies to structure national economies.

In fact, however, learning is not about strategic choices of best practices. Even at the company level, learning is very conditional: Japanese-style lean production looks very different in Germany than it does in the United States. Institutions can constrain and/or support strategies and practices, but the reverse is true as well—strategies and practices can also affect institutions. It remains as important to ask who has the power to exercise strategic choices as it does to determine how these choices can be exercised and how people think about them.

Finally, we need to add to our explanatory framework not just institutions, organizations, and the strategies and practices that make sense within the contexts they establish, but also the ways in which entrenched ideologies (often translated into strategies) may not reflect any natural interests of either employers or the collective representatives of labor. Differing ideas—for example, about best practice or appropriate ways of negotiating conflicting interests—can both energize learning by offering breadth and impede it when certain potentially constructive ideas are ruled out. This added dimension is so extraordinarily difficult to define that we do not attempt to do so. However, it can be discerned throughout the dynamics we analyze here. While it is the least developed dimension of our comparative studies, we certainly do not regard it as the least important.

THE CHAPTERS

Since the 1990s, social scientists have often placed Germany and the United States at more or less opposite ends of a conceptual continuum, with the institutionally coordinated German Social Market Economy and its employment relations system at one end and the U.S. political economy, with its decentralized system of labor–management relations, at the other. We try to play on the strengths of this heuristic without getting caught up in it, staying open to ways in which it may not fit the comparison. By pointing up strengths and weaknesses at each end, these chapters throw curves, possibly loops, into the conceptual continuum.

We develop the German-American comparison by placing employment relations side-by-side with related areas of political economic activity. This contextualization is unconventional. It does not systematically examine the role of the state or the historical development of institutions; neither does it offer traditional sectoral comparisons of employment relations. Therefore, we sacrifice some theoretical elegance, analytical precision, and breadth of comparison. However, we gain something we believe is more important: a sometimes messy but empirically rich examination of key arenas of political economic change, each of which either directly or indirectly influences and reflects industrial and employment relations in the two countries. Taking four different points of departure, we focus on the intersection between the strategies and practices of employers, unions, and employer associations (among other actors) and the cultural and institutional frameworks within which they operate.

Chapter 2, by Rosemary Batt and Owen Darbishire, analyzes the deregulation and privatization of the telecommunications industries in the United States and Germany, emphasizing the interplay between organizational and institutional change and labor–management relations. Batt and Darbishire place the break-up of AT&T and the deregulation and privatization of Deutsche Telekom at opposite ends of a continuum. At the U.S. end of the continuum we see virtually no political constraints on private-sector strategies. In Germany, however, the Postal Workers Union succeeded in slowing organizational change and protecting workers in the process. In both cases, but especially in Germany, it is not clear that consumers have benefited substantially from the reorganization of the industry. However, it is clear that in Germany labor has not (yet?) become a "loser" in this transformation, while the U.S. change has resulted in mass layoffs and a weakening of the unions. Nevertheless, significant variations in labor–management relations and negotiations within this sector in the United States illustrate a relatively wide range of possible outcomes.

David Finegold and Brent Keltner's chapter on management development (Chapter 3) draws attention to how the strengths of each country are mirrored by weaknesses in the other. The authors argue that the Germans are good at providing a high floor of technical competence in managerial development. They also show, however, that functional specialization and organizational rigidity are supported by narrowly defined university training curricula as well as management career paths. In the United States, by contrast, we find broadly skilled managers who are flexibly deployed in organizations. However, in smaller firms, the quality of management development (especially in technical areas) is highly uneven, and the "floor" of management skills is lower than in Germany. This chapter sheds light on the advantages and disadvantages of each country's institutions and approaches to management as a field, and thus management development.

In Chapter 4, Steven Casper compares two efforts at mutual learning and innovation in the area of supplier relations. He analyzes the implementation of Japanese just-in-time (JIT) inventory systems in Germany and the United States and the significant implications for changing relationships among firms. In Germany, we learn just how cumbersome institutional change can be in the face of preexisting legal arrangements of corporate governance. In the United States, Casper shows the obstacles to the diffusion of innovations such as JIT in a setting in which corporate law allows private sector firms far greater latitude than in Germany. Both the concerted employer action in Germany and the company-by-company strategies in the United States have advantages and disadvantages, and here again, variations within each country suggest learning possibilities not just between the two countries but among industries and even firms within them.

Finally, in Chapter 5, Lowell Turner, Michael Fichter, and I examine contemporary employment relations in the two countries. Because employment relations are so deeply embedded in national and lower-level institutional structures, this chapter follows from the others and most clearly illustrates the interconnected nature of the various facets of the two political economies. We characterize Germany as struggling with a crisis of the "high road": high wages, high-level skills, and high labor-value-added in a highly institutionalized labor market. The United States faces a crisis of the "low road," with relatively stagnant wages, income inequality, continuing union decline, and highly fragmented and competing systems of employment relations embedded in an extremely diverse political economy. Given the very different nature of the problems facing the two countries, we suggest very different policy prescriptions for approaching those crises, based in large measure on the mirror image conceptualization noted earlier.

The political economic spheres of activity analyzed here either directly involve or are closely interwoven with the relationship between labor and employers. Batt and Darbishire, in their chapter on telecommunications, explicitly analyze the impact on labor–management relations of this sector's reorganization. Finegold and Keltner's chapter on management training systems in the two countries has indirect but critical importance for employment relations, because the way managers are trained has a great deal to do with how organizations are run. How managers are trained can not be disentangled from the content and effectiveness of management's labor and human resource strategies. Relations among employers, such as the supplier relations analyzed by Casper, tell us a great deal about the functioning of different versions of capitalism (e.g., the social market versus the free market variant). These differences have important implications for the scope of collective action in labor–management relations. Finally, the Turner, Fichter, and Wever analysis of employment relations in Chapter 5 explains how labor, management, and the employment relationship shape and reflect their political economic contexts.

TRADE-OFFS

Powerful social actors cannot afford to and/or do not want to wait for national political processes to solve urgent political economic problems; but they can benefit from the mutual learning process, and—as the chapters of this volume show—to some extent they do. Yet there remains much to be done. The German telecommunications industry still appears far too constrained by the nature and tenor of labor–management relations to meet customers' needs. Institutional change, such as the introduction of JIT, is hampered by the legal arrangements of corporate governance. Functional specialization and organizational rigidity within firms are supported by narrowly defined university training curricula and management career paths. German employment relations severely tax many struggling companies in the eastern states and, increasingly, smaller companies in the west. The U.S. case also offers a mixed picture. As the JIT story illustrates, the lack of mechanisms in the United States for coordinating employers' actions is not in their collective interest. Telecommunications deregulation has forced more rapid firm-level adjustment than has been possible in Germany, but the economy has also suffered from a lack of industry-wide coordination, which has in turn led to arguably unnecessary technological investments and to suboptimal outcomes for labor and customers. Especially in smaller U.S. firms, the uneven quality of management development (particularly in technical areas) results in substantial measure from the lack of coordinated skills and training standards above the level of the individual firm. Perhaps the most glaring example of the problems associated with a lack of institutional framework supports is found in employment relations and the resulting stagnant wages, income inequality, union decline, and associated social problems.

In many regards, the U.S.-German comparison suggests an analogy, with the strengths of each country reflected in the weaknesses of the other. While the U.S. economy is doing well by macroeconomic indicators, the social costs of U.S.-style growth are significant. If the German social fabric remains fairly stable, fears about competitiveness, especially in the high-technology and service sectors, combined with continuing high levels of unemployment, present the opposite picture: social stability at high economic cost. There appears to be a trade-off between the so-called employment miracle of the United States and the relatively more even distribution of wealth and income (in part due to a significant social wage) in the German social market economy.

We find evidence of trade-offs in each of the instances of political economic change analyzed in this volume. As illustrated by Batt and Darbishire, in the German telecommunications industry, workers continue to maintain high levels of employment. However, Deutsche Telekom has been extremely slow to adopt new technologies and organizational strategies, such that services long considered standard in the United States remain limited or unavailable to German customers. On the other hand, rapid technological and organizational change in the United States have benefited (especially business) consumers while entailing considerable wage and work-rule concessions and mass layoffs among the industry's workers.

The trade-off with respect to management development systems in the two countries leaves most German firms with technically competent but functionally specialized managers, as shown by Finegold and Keltner. The high floor of technical competence appears to be gained at the cost of the development of broadly skilled managers who could be deployed cross-functionally in high-performance organizations (see, for example, Applebaum and Batt 1994; Berg 1997). In the United States, by contrast, high-performance innovation is common in companies with strong market positions, while smaller, less competitive firms are left to choose from a labor market pool of managers with relatively low skill levels, especially in the area of technical competence.

A similar contrast emerges in Casper's analysis of supplier relations. Here again, German institutional rigidities, in this instance in the form of legal frameworks structuring interfirm relations, create barriers to innovations in how suppliers and final producers distribute the risks associated with the introduction of JIT. The relatively unconstrained nature of interfirm contracting relationships in the United States stands in marked contrast. However, the result in the United States is that weaker market players, in this case supplier firms, are to some extent forced to accept the terms of stronger final assemblers. While some U.S. assemblers have developed stable, long-term relations with suppliers that mitigate some of the effects of this imbalance of market power, many have not. Meanwhile, historically rooted legal frameworks in Germany work to protect suppliers at the expense of end producers to the extent that the former require on-site inspection of supplied parts at delivery—precisely the sort of time-consuming process that JIT is designed to avoid. As Casper points out, the familiar institutional rigidity/market flexibility trade-off holds in this arena as well. The coordinated innovation of new legal frameworks within trade associations in the German electronics industry (now apparently diffusing to other industries) represents an exception rather than a rule.

Finally, the trade-off appears as one between stability and innovation in Chapter 5 on employment relations. The segmented U.S. system, with multiple competing models of industrial, labor, and employment relations, is characterized by everything from internationally impressive innovations in labor–management partnerships to low-trust, low-skill, low-wage cases and industries. Strong market players can hire and retain skilled workers or train workers that they hire. They can also develop high-performance work organizations that capitalize on workers' skills, including their ability to participate directly in management decision making, which in turn bolsters these companies' overall competitiveness. Smaller and/or weaker companies, often lacking the resources to train workers adequately, and often confronting a labor pool of relatively unskilled workers (or workers whose skills do not match their needs), are generally unable to pursue what Turner, Fichter, and I call "high-road" employment strategies. This further weakens their overall market position. Workers may "win" if they are employed by "winning" companies or, in some cases, if they are represented by unions that can induce firms to pursue high-road strategies.

Undoubtedly some of these are unavoidable trade-offs between a socially negotiated and a more unilateral market-oriented approach to political economic change and adjustment. However, it does not follow that anything gained by mutual learning entails an equal and opposite loss. In the cases analyzed here, we find both necessary trade-offs and trade-offs that may simply reflect articles of ideological faith that are difficult to alter but are not in any way naturally determined. We hope that this book will help illustrate how these trade-offs can be finessed. To do so, actors in each country will have to pay closer attention to the difference between institutional constraints—ideologically unacceptable in the United States and increasingly onerous to some social actors in Germany—and institutional supports. Such supports provide at least the potential for balancing social and economic interests, as illustrated by Germany's spectacular postwar economic miracle.

The Germans are probably at an advantage in that they already have in place a set of institutions that can contain debates about new and emerging issues of substantive change. For instance, regional collective bargaining among employer associations and large industrial unions provides a forum for renegotiating which issues will be hammered out between individual firms and their works councils and which will be negotiated at the meso-level. In the United States, local and regional actors in a few places have begun to create such institutions but these are as yet young and far from robust (Parker 1997). Yet in a different way, the United States is in a better position than Germany: Americans seem to have a peculiar talent for seeing the need for change, reorganizing and recombining resources (including human resources) to accommodate shifting contexts, and then remaining open and flexible. It remains to be seen which—if either—of these comparative fortés is more conducive to learning.

Notes

1. *Neue Länder* is the German term for the new states of the former East Germany.
2. Employers "poach" when they hire employees away from firms that have already invested in their training, thus effectively stealing their competitors' investments in human resources.

References

Applebaum, Eileen, and Rosemary Batt. 1994. *The New American Workplace: Transforming Work Systems in the United States*. Ithaca, New York: ILR Press, Cornell University.

Berg, Peter. 1997. *Fostering High-Performance Work Systems in Germany and the United States*. Unpublished conference paper, Economic Policy Institute, Washington, D.C.

Berger, Suzanne, and Michael Piore. 1980. *Dualism and Discontinuity in Industrial Societies*. Cambridge: Cambridge University Press.

Dore, Ronald. 1973. *British Factory—Japanese Factory: The Origins of National Diversity in Industrial Relations*. London: Allen and Unwin.

Hamel, Gary, and C.K. Prahalad. 1994. *Competing for the Future: Breakthrough Strategies for Seizing Control of Your Industry and Creating the Markets of Tomorrow*. Boston: Harvard Business School Press.

Hyman, Richard. 1994. "Introduction: Economic Restructuring, Market Liberalism and the Future of Industrial Relations Systems." In *New Frontiers in European Industrial Relations*, Richard Hyman and Anthony Ferner, eds. London: Blackwell Press.

Jacoby, Wade. 1997. "Learning, Tinkering or Building? Speculations on Institutional Transfer in Advanced Economics." Working paper, Grinell College, Political Science Department, Grinell, Iowa.

Kotter, James, and William Heskett. 1992. *Corporate Culture*. Boston: Harvard Business School Press.

Lane, Christel. 1989. *Management and Labour in Europe*. Aldershot, England: Edward Elgar.

Maurice, Marc, Francois Sellier, and Jean-Jacques Sylvestre. 1986. *The Social Foundations of Industrial Power: A Comparison on France and Germany*. Cambridge: MIT Press.

Naisbitt, John. 1997. *Megatrends Asia*. New York: Simon and Schuster.

Parker, Eric. 1997. "Regional Industrial Revitalization: Implications for Workforce Development Policy." Working paper no. 114, Center for Urban Policy Research, Rutgers University, New Brunswick, New Jersey.

Porter, Michael. 1998. *The Competitive Advantage of Nations*. Boston: Harvard Business School Press.

Thelen, Kathleen. 1991. *Union of Parts: Labor Politics in Postwar Germany*. Ithaca, New York: Cornell University Press.

Turner, Lowell. 1991. *Democracy at Work: Changing World Markets and the Future of Labor Unions*. Ithaca, New York: Cornell University Press.

Walgenbach, Peter. 1993. "Führungsverhalten mittlerer Manager in Deutschland und Grossbritannien" (Leadership among Middle Managers in Germany and Great Britain). *ZEW Newsletter* 2: pp. 17–21 (Zentrum für Europäische Wirtschaftsforschung).

Wever, Kirsten S. 1995. *Negotiating Competitiveness: Employment Relations and Organizational Innovation in Germany and the United States*. Boston: Harvard Business School Press.

Womack, James P., Daniel T. Jones, and Daniel Roos. 1991. *The Machine That Changed the World: The Story of Lean Production*. New York: HarperCollins.

2

Deregulation and Restructuring in Telecommunications Services in the United States and Germany

Rosemary Batt
Cornell University

Owen Darbishire
University of Oxford

The telecommunications services industry provides a particularly useful and interesting lens for considering the issue of mutual learning between the United States and Germany. As noted in Chapter 1 to this volume, most learning in the field of industrial relations has tended to be a one-way street, with U.S. researchers and practitioners advocating the replication of successful components of the "German model," such as the apprenticeship system or works councils, which undergird high levels of skill and productivity in manufacturing. The experience of the telecommunications industry, however, provides the opportunity for Germany also to learn from the United States because the United States continues to lead the world in providing high-quality universal service. Mutual learning is particularly important in this industry because it employs 1–2 percent of the workforce in both countries (Katz 1997) and provides a critical infrastructure for the competitiveness of firms and "information-based" economies.

Historically and currently, the leadership role of the United States in telecommunications grows out of its technological innovations, with early pioneering work in information technologies and systems engineering at AT&T's Bell Labs and with the later deployment of cellular, satellite, and other advanced technologies by new entrants such as Microwave Communications Inc. (MCI). The availability of alternative wireless communications systems from MCI and others, in turn, convinced U.S. regulators that the AT&T monopoly was not viable, leading to deregulation of the long-distance and equipment markets by 1984.[1] In response to deregulation and new low-cost competitors, AT&T reoriented its corporate strategies and structures to serve differentiated market segments, invested heavily in fiber-optic cable and digital transmission and switching systems, and reengineered operating systems. These innovations brought significant cost reductions in equipment and long-distance service; dramatic improvements in response time, quality, and speed of transmission; and diversity of product offerings. Business customers, who were heavy users of equipment and long distance, particularly benefited. In anticipation of local deregulation (finally legislated in 1996), the regional Bell operating companies (RBOCs) mimicked AT&T's strategies. The U.S. case, therefore, serves as an example of how organizational restructuring improved performance of an industry that is vital to national economic competitiveness (both directly and as an important input into other goods- and service-producing industries).

By contrast, in spite of a historically high level of technological competence within Deutsche Telekom (Telekom), the nature and path of adjustment in response to the pressures of competition and reform have been significantly different, and slower. Deutsche Telekom was privatized in 1994 but still retained a monopoly in providing telephone and cable TV. Deployment of digital systems considerably lags behind that in the United States, and consumers receive slower service and fewer product offerings and pay higher prices. Telekom has struggled to reorganize itself by copying the corporate strategies, organizational structures, and work practices of U.S. firms.

Because of the slower pace of reform, however, Telekom also stands to learn from the mistakes made in the United States, where deregulation has led to increased inequality among consumers and workers. For consumers, the restructuring has benefited businesses because they no longer pay rates that subsidize universal residential service. Both business and high-end retail customers can take advantage of falling prices for long-distance calling, high-speed networks, or enhanced features such as voice messaging. For lower-income consumers, however, the basic costs of local service have risen, and these consumers are less likely to be able to take advantage of new products or enhanced features, even if they are less costly than before (Keefe and Boroff 1994, p. 318). For labor, restructuring has not only displaced employees and reduced union strength, but it has also created more unequal labor market conditions both within and between union and nonunion segments. To the extent that Germany wishes to preserve equality for consumers and workers, this chapter provides an analysis of how inequality in U.S. outcomes has occurred.

The United States stands to learn from Germany as well. In response to real and anticipated deregulation, former Bell companies downsized rapidly, depleting their embedded skill base, demoralizing their workforce, and paying large severance or early retirement packages. As an unintended consequence, those packages subsidized the labor costs of competitors because competitors often hired former Bell employees whose pension and health insurance were already covered by their retirement packages. Moreover, from 1996 on, Bell companies failed to anticipate the explosion in demand for Internet access and new products, and they found themselves understaffed and scrambling to fill vacancies for skilled employees.[2] This chapter demonstrates how the slower pace and continued monopoly status of Telekom allowed it the opportunity to retrain its workforce and shift employees from traditional to growth segments of the market without incurring the substantial costs of turnover and displacement, which negatively affect both management and labor.

These differences in paths to restructuring are more striking because U.S. and German telecommunications monopolists have quite similar starting points. This similarity is in contrast to manufacturing, where mass-production systems in the United States were considerably more developed than in Germany. Historically, most countries operated public telephone monopolies with quite similar organizational structures. These companies were highly regulated, quasi-public enterprises providing a basic service to the public. While Deutsche Telekom operated as part of the Bundespost, which included the national post, bank, and telecommunications, under the auspices of the Federal Minister of Posts and Telecommunications, AT&T was regulated by the (functionally similar) Federal Communications Commission (FCC). Generally, telephone companies were large bureaucratic organizations offering lifetime employment with high wages and benefits to employees who either considered themselves public servants or who were officially part of the civil service. In other words, the internal labor market rules governing work and employment relations in different countries (beyond just the United States and Germany) appear to have been remarkably similar. Equally, unionization rates in the industry were very high among eligible workers. Under these circumstances, one might expect the United States, Germany, and other countries to follow similar paths to deregulation, with similar corporate strategic responses and stakeholder outcomes.

Other unique features of the industry argue for the adoption of parallel adjustment paths among countries. To be globally competitive, most former national telecommunications monopolies need to pursue, and have pursued, joint ventures in order to enter each others' markets, such as AT&T with its World Partners and Deutsche Telekom with France Télécom and Sprint. These companies are laying global networks of cable to provide integrated voice, video, and data services to worldwide customers. The integrated nature, or "systemness," of network technology requires compatibility of systems across regional and national boundaries. Moreover, because of the concentrated structure of the industry in each country, in which former monopolists continue to be the dominant players, the strategic choices of a handful of players significantly shape the direction of industrial change. The key players, who include Deutsche Telekom, AT&T, and the regional Bell operating companies in the United States, closely watch and learn from each other's experience. In contrast to manufacturing, where decentralized production units are more viable, this predilection to watch and learn again increases the likelihood that the transfer of technology and the borrowing of work organization strategies among countries will be substantial.

Yet in spite of the similarity of initial starting points and underlying pressures for change, the trajectory of the telecommunications industry in the United States and Germany has diverged. We argue that the different paths of restructuring in the two countries reflect classic underlying differences in governance structures and industrial relations systems. There is also variation within the United States, however, which reflects the weak institutionalization and fragmentation in government regulatory bodies and labor market institutions at the national and state levels. Thus, we argue that differences in national and regional industrial relations systems play a central role, both in shaping regulatory policy and in shaping corporate strategy and work organization. These alternative approaches, in turn, lead to significantly different outcomes for stakeholders: consumers, firms, employees, and unions. We distinguish cases along a continuum from the highly unconstrained, "market-driven" example of AT&T, to the intermediate "consumer-driven" cases of two RBOCs, to the highly constrained, "labor-mediated" approach of Germany.

On the product market side, deregulation and reregulation are the result of political contests within existing institutional structures and are therefore not exogenous. In the AT&T case, market reform was evolutionary and did not occur through legislative or "overtly political" action. Rather, MCI, backed by corporate constituents, used the FCC and the courts to create a "free market." In an interesting twist on the historic use of the courts to undermine labor's power, the MCI coalition used the courts to undermine the power of the unionized employer and create a nonunion alternative. The resulting policy was one of "regulatory asymmetry" that privileged new entrants, ensured that AT&T would lose market share, and prohibited former Bell system companies from entering certain product markets (local and cable TV in the case of AT&T and long distance, equipment, and cable TV in the case of the RBOCs). This structure, in turn, created the incentive for reregulated Bell companies to shift the costs of restructuring to their unionized workforce. In sum, the evolutionary transformation of the product market was a response to corporate constituents who pushed in a pluralistic (or fragmented) institutional environment not for complete market deregulation but for reregulation that would favor new entrants.

In contrast to AT&T, the RBOCs enjoyed a longer time horizon and more favorable conditions for restructuring because they served local markets, which were not as lucrative for new entrants. More importantly, politically elected regulators and legislators were concerned about the potential negative effects of restructuring on the mass of citizen consumers—their political base. The RBOCs were and continue to be regulated by state Public Utility Commissions (PUCs), elected bodies whose purpose is to keep rates low for consumers and to ensure universal service. Product-market liberalization occurred incrementally, on a state-by-state basis. In exchange for guarantees of low rates and continued quality service, some state PUCs replaced fixed rates with more market-oriented, "incentive" rates—rates that allowed RBOCs to retain some of the profits from efficiency-enhancing innovations. In the two cases here, BellSouth was successful in this strategy in all of its nine states, while NYNEX[3] was not. In addition, rather than oppose deregulation as AT&T had done, all of the RBOCs united to use their political strength in states and communities across the country to gain U.S. Congressional support for a version of deregulation that favored incumbent local providers, the bill that finally passed in 1996.

In the German case, it was the powerful Deutsche Postgewerkschaft (DPG) union that successfully pressured the national government to approach deregulation at a much slower and more cautious pace and in ways that have privileged and protected Deutsche Telekom in the intervening period. In this case, the "regulatory asymmetry," which favors Telekom and the unionized workforce, is not a response to business (as in the AT&T case) or to consumers (as in the RBOC case), but to labor. As Germany privatizes and deregulates the telecommunications industry, for example, Telekom has been allowed to continue monopoly control of the cable TV market, potentially giving it a substantial strategic and competitive advantage. The DPG was able to exercise significant influence and protect employee and union interests because it operated in a neocorporatist framework within a "semi-sovereign state" (Katzenstein 1987). That is, within the German system, political power is dispersed between large, encompassing social groups and decentralized states. The integration of peak economic interests into the formulation of economic policy constrains unilateral decision making and promotes cooperation and consensus. Privatization and reregulation have, consequently, occurred in a framework designed to perpetuate union and employee rights.

Differences in labor market institutions and managerial strategic choice provide a parallel story. AT&T's market-driven approach has been characterized by unilateral action on the part of management, a failure to jointly develop work reorganization strategies, and a reliance on technology and reengineering, rather than human resource strategies, to achieve organizational reform and competitiveness. As a result, the workforce has borne the major costs of restructuring. The restrictions on entering new markets, coupled with the economies of scale of new technology and cost pressures from new nonunion entrants, led AT&T to downsize its nonmanagement workforce by 60 percent and the management workforce by 30 percent in a decade.

The RBOCs have imitated many of AT&T's strategies, but with a longer time horizon and under the constraints of state PUCs. While the mission of the PUCs is not to protect union or workers' rights, unions have been able to leverage the concern of the PUCs for consumer welfare to gain decisions that also benefit workers. For example, unions have united with consumer groups to block rate reform unless accompanied by higher staffing levels to ensure good customer service. They also have induced the RBOCs to agree to union rights in their new subsidiaries in exchange for not opposing RBOC petitions before state utility commissions. Thus, the strategic use of PUC oversight by unions has had an indirect positive effect on worker welfare and union rights, an effect that varies among states.

The German approach, by contrast, has been a "mutualist," or labor-mediated, one. The DPG has slowed the pace of deregulation while simultaneously seeking to protect union and employee interests through detailed involvement and participation in the reorganization of work and corporate structures. Equally, until late 1995, the DPG restricted the possibility of downsizing, while it also influenced corporate strategies to encourage the development of an expanded range of services to ease the impact of digitalization on the workforce. However, the slower pace has translated into slower adoption of new technologies, work practices, and corporate structures. The quality and availability of new services has suffered. Consequently, consumers rather than workers have absorbed more of the costs of restructuring. The remainder of this chapter elaborates the details of the above argument by presenting the evidence of the U.S. cases and the German case. Comparative analysis and conclusions for mutual learning follow.

THE UNITED STATES

The events surrounding the breakup of the Bell System in 1984 have been well documented (Coll 1986; Temin 1987; Stone 1989; Teske 1990; Cohen 1992). The attack on AT&T's monopoly was in response to a series of regulatory decisions, in the 1940s through 1960s, which meant that AT&T's high long-distance rates were increasingly subsidizing local calls. This created an incentive for new competitors to enter the lucrative long-distance market, offering services at costs lower than AT&T but above "market-clearing" prices. After winning a 1969 lawsuit that allowed it to provide private-line services, MCI spent the next decade building an anti-AT&T coalition comprising other new entrants, the computer industry led by IBM, and major corporate users, particularly multinational financial services and airline corporations (Aronson and Cowhey 1988; Teske 1990; Cohen 1992). A series of FCC decisions in the 1970s, coupled with court rulings which favored the anti-AT&T coalition, progressively undermined the structure of the Bell system.

Divestiture occurred with very little political support. Over 70 percent of telephone customers opposed the 1984 breakup of the Bell system (Keefe and Boroff 1994, p. 316), as did state PUCs and independent telephone companies.[4] Even the Reagan administration opposed the breakup. However, the pluralistic structure of the U.S. government meant that "interested parties could approach that part of the government most sympathetic to their cause" (Temin 1987, p. 341). In the early 1980s, MCI, IBM, and business customers achieved their goals through the Department of Justice and the courts, having become frustrated with Congress and temporarily blocked by the FCC.

The court order that dismantled the Bell system in 1984 responded to the interests of the anti-AT&T coalition: MCI and other alternative providers gained access to long-distance markets; multinational corporate users obtained reductions in the cost of long distance and equipment inputs. AT&T retained its long-distance and equipment operation but was forced to compete in a system of "asymmetric regulation," which ensured that AT&T's long-distance market share dropped steadily. By 1994, this share amounted to 60 percent (FCC 1992/1993). AT&T's 22 local telephone companies were merged into the seven RBOC monopolies, which were barred from participation in equipment production. They could only enter other markets providing they did not use their monopoly position to do so.

Stakeholders, such as unions, employees, and residential customers, were entirely excluded from the deregulatory process and were unable to promote either the status quo or the security of union institutions, a sharp contrast to Germany. In spite of the fact that Bell system employees numbered over one million, or almost 1 percent of the U.S.

workforce, neither job security nor the future of collective bargaining structures was addressed in the divestiture process (Darbishire 1997b).

In the following sections, we assess the variation in processes and outcomes of restructuring in the cases of AT&T and of the RBOCs BellSouth and NYNEX, to illustrate how variation in product and labor market institutions have shaped firm strategies and stakeholder outcomes. The variation reflects differences in the extent and rapidity of deregulation, differences between local and long-distance product markets, and differences in the political embeddedness of the enterprises and union strategic responses. More fundamentally, the extent of variation reflects the fact that institutions such as labor unions and employee and consumer groups that might have strengthened the positions of their members were weak, and this weakness left room for substantial managerial prerogative in shaping reregulation.

AT&T

The AT&T case represents a strong example of managerial prerogative in which the company focused on converting itself from a public service bureaucracy to a lean, sales-maximizing global enterprise. Three factors shaped AT&T's business and labor strategy during this period: its strategic focus on global over domestic markets, its lack of political constraints or local service requirements, and its need to immediately compete in an asymmetrical regulatory environment against new low-cost competitors such as MCI and Sprint. Union influence on AT&T's strategy has been limited to maintaining high relative wages and negotiating generous severance and early retirement packages in exchange for labor peace. Although joint labor–management work-design initiatives received considerable publicity in the 1990s, they had little impact on actual management practices.

First, with respect to globalization, AT&T focused on the "natural" extension of its long-distance market and leveraged this competitive advantage to create international networks, reshaping itself into a global corporation. Global service means providing an integrated set of voice, data, and video services though a seamless international network, particularly for multinational businesses. This global strategy has included political efforts to reduce international trade barriers, including a strong push to deregulate public monopolies in all countries. The RBOCs, by contrast, have entered international markets by leveraging their expertise in local service provision to form joint ventures with national monopolists to improve basic services, particularly in developing countries.

Second, AT&T and the RBOC's historic division of the long-distance and local market within the United States means that AT&T largely has indirect contact with its massive customer base. AT&T's long-distance service is provided through access to local networks operated by the RBOCs, who themselves have a more direct and ongoing relationship with customers. AT&T continues to be regulated by the FCC, but it does not have political ties to states or regions and is not constrained by state PUCs. AT&T has taken advantage of its national structure to consolidate and move operations to whatever location offers the lowest cost. The RBOCs, by contrast, cannot move operations out of their state jurisdictions without state PUC approval.

Finally, in 1984 (just after the deregulation of the long-distance and equipment markets), AT&T immediately began competing against new nonunion, low-cost entrants in long distance in the asymmetric regulatory environment. The cost advantages of these new competitors derived from the following: they did not inherit bureaucratic organizational structures, they began with more maintenance-free technologies, they did not have sunk costs in obsolete technologies or have to reengineer complex systems, and they were operating with a younger, nonunion workforce with labor costs of roughly half those of the Bell companies.

To respond to these cost pressures, AT&T reorganized into cross-functional business units targeting distinct market segments: large business, small business, and residential customers. To achieve segmented marketing strategies, business unit reorganization, and geographic consolidation, AT&T relied primarily on its traditional strengths of technology and engineering to achieve economies of scale rather than on human resource strategies. It anticipated significant gains in cross-functional coordination through reengineered information systems that flow horizontally. These technology and reengineering strategies were designed to maximize the multiple goals of reducing costs, increasing the speed and quality of transmission, expanding the variety of services offered, and improving response time.

On the network side, AT&T upgraded its long-distance network by replacing copper with fiber-optic cable and completing the digitalization of switching and transmission systems. Together these technologies created a system that is largely maintenance-free and has greater capacity to transmit voice, video, data, and higher quality service. Digitalization allows employees to remotely diagnose and repair network systems. This capability has reduced the demand for blue-collar craft workers with high levels of traditional electromechanical skills. They have been replaced by a much smaller number of white-collar computer specialists and systems analysts and a much larger number of computer-monitoring clerks paid at 80 percent of former craft wages. Central office switching was consolidated into two major centers—one serving customers east of the Mississippi and one serving those to the west, plus a handful of remote regional centers (MacDuffie and Maccoby 1986).

On the sales and service side, AT&T cut costs and labor by consolidating hundreds of local operator and customer service offices into a handful of remote national centers with toll-free phone access. Rather than reduce Taylorism,[5] it has used new computer and software information systems to create repetitive jobs that are machine-paced, electronically monitored, and functionally specialized. This strategy, however, varies significantly by market segment. Automatic call distribution systems determine the call volume of customers and automatically link them to the appropriate labor market segment. College-educated managers handle large business customers and provide on-site, "one-stop shopping." Nonmanagement service consultants serve small business customers, handling 25–30 calls per day. Residential service reps serve the mass of consumers; unlike "universal service reps" of the past, these employees are now functionally specialized into sales, billing, collections, and repair. Furthermore, they are tied to computers driven by expert systems and handle roughly 80–90 calls per day. Management and union representatives alike agree that these have become the most stressful jobs in the industry because of intense pressure to sell, to handle customers courteously, and to turn over calls quickly, all within the context of ongoing electronic monitoring.

In sum, the market segmentation strategy increases inequality in service among customer segments according to the ability to pay; the strategy also increases labor market segmentation within companies, as the design of jobs, skill requirements, and wage levels are equated to the customer segment being served (see Batt 2000a for a broader discussion of these segmentation strategies and outcomes). This segmentation strategy, coupled with the downward pressure on wages from nonunion competitors, particularly at the lower end, has led to increased labor market inequality within occupations, companies, and the industry as a whole. Between 1984 and 1994, for example, wage inequality within customer services more than tripled (Batt and Strausser 1998; Batt and Keefe 1999).

Two additional effects of these strategies on the workforce have been paramount: labor displacement and declining morale. While initially viewed as a temporary strategy, downsizing became an increasingly routine part of business for AT&T in the decade following deregulation. AT&T reduced its domestic nonmanagement workforce by 60 percent between 1984 and 1995 (from 250,000 to 100,000); it reduced management ranks by 33 percent.[6] As downsizing continued, involuntary rather than voluntary separations came to represent an increasing proportion of the terminations, with later rounds of downsizing offering employees smaller severance or early retirement packages. In the first two years of postdivestiture operations, for example, AT&T reduced its head count by 56,000 positions. Only 25 percent involved layoffs; the remainder left through attrition, voluntary severance, early retirement, transfers within AT&T, or transfers back to the RBOCs. Between 1984 and 1992, 58 percent of separations in the unionized workforce involved layoffs, while 42 percent involved voluntary separations. In the company's 1996 announcement of another round of downsizing, it indicated that most separations would occur through layoffs (see Keefe and Batt 1997).

For the survivor workforce, restructuring has had profound effects on morale. While in 1981, 68 percent of the nonmanagement employees felt that the company provided job security and only 8 percent did not, by 1991, the opposite was true: 73 percent said there was little job security while less than 4 percent felt there was any job security. Sixty-six percent felt unable to affect the course of events at AT&T, and 80 percent had little confidence in management's ability to lead the corporation (Keefe and Batt 1997). Career opportunities also fell. Whereas in the past, employees would follow job ladders in local communities, now they often had to move their families across the country to accept promotion opportunities. A 1991 study surveyed workers who had survived several rounds of downsizing at AT&T. Those workers whose jobs had been "surplused" (eliminated) and who had stayed at AT&T by transferring to other positions found themselves in the "surplus" status on average 2.5 times in a five-year period (Keefe and Boroff 1994, p. 328). Some 87 percent of the survey respondents said they wanted to keep their current jobs until they retired, but less than 10 percent believed that there was any opportunity for advancement at AT&T (Keefe and Boroff 1994, p. 328).

AT&T's cost-cutting labor strategy also included shifting from a predominantly unionized (67 percent) workforce in 1984 to a predominantly nonunionized one (42 percent) in 1995. This was accomplished by downsizing the unionized core, expanding the workforce in nonunion enterprises, and increasing the number of management job titles, which are ineligible for union representation. AT&T established two nonunion subsidiaries, American Transtech (the largest U.S. telemarketing service) and AT&T Universal Card (the second largest U.S. credit card company). It acquired two nonunion equipment manufacturers, Paradyne (data communications equipment) and National Cash Register (NCR). American Transtech and NCR were subsequently spun off as separate companies. In addition, new jobs requiring more technical or professional skills related to new technologies were often defined as managerial and exempt from union representation. As a result, the percentage of the workforce defined as managerial grew from 29 percent in 1984 to over 50 percent in 1995 (Keefe and Batt 1997).

Labor–management relations, historically cooperative, collapsed under these pressures, as did the Quality of Worklife (QWL) program negotiated in 1980. Beginning in the late 1980s, AT&T initiated some joint union–management experiments in total quality management (TQM) and self-managed teams. However, most fell apart in the 1990s when the company initiated downsizing and reengineering, which undermined employee morale and the stable relationships between workers and managers necessary to make these innovations successful. In 1992, a negotiated pact, "Workplace of the Future," was designed to reestablish cooperative labor–management relations by involving the union and workers in work innovations at several levels of the organization, from the strategic business units to the workplace. Successful adoption, however, depended on managerial choice at decentralized business units, and few managers chose to participate. Today, many managers, workers, and trade unionists remain highly skeptical about top management's commitment to this effort. They cite AT&T's history of presenting positive public relations images but not following through on the implementation.

The Regional Bell Companies:
BellSouth and NYNEX

The political debate and approach to regulatory reform surrounding the RBOCs has been considerably different than that for AT&T because of the RBOCs' central role in providing basic universal service. The issue of consumer welfare figured more prominently in the debate over deregulating local markets among both national and state officials, and as elected officials responded to their constituents, labor often benefited as an unintended consequence. While long-distance service is viewed as unessential, local service is considered a necessity for emergency medical and life-threatening circumstances. Because costs exceed revenues in local service, regulators historically ensured universal service by requiring AT&T to help subsidize local service by paying an access fee to connect to the local Bell infrastructure, a requirement extended to all long-distance companies after 1984.

The central problem in local service deregulation, therefore, was to figure out how to ensure continued universal access, particularly in small towns and rural areas. A "free market" solution would have resulted in dramatic price increases for basic service, an unacceptable political solution. This, in fact, did occur as a result of long-distance deregulation, where long-distance rates dropped by 40 percent and call volume doubled, but basic residential rates increased by more than 60 percent—from $11.58 to $18.66 (Keefe and Boroff 1994, p. 318).[7]

The RBOCs, therefore, continued their monopoly in local service in the decade after divestiture while regulators considered alternative solutions. This longer time horizon also benefited consumers as well as employees by allowing the RBOCs to reduce their workforce through attrition, early retirement offerings, or through retraining and replacement in growth sides of the business, particularly cellular. Finally in 1996, a politically powerful RBOC coalition successfully pushed through its version of legislative reform in the U.S. Congress, a "fast track" version that favored incumbent providers over AT&T, MCI, and new entrants. In this version, local companies could offer long-distance service as soon as they opened their markets to competitors; but because of their established base, the RBOCs were considered to have a competitive advantage. Moreover, in May 1997, FCC regulators finally issued rules to handle the cross-subsidy problem. While a comprehensive agreement on universal service was not reached, an initial compromise gave the RBOCs transition time by phasing in reductions in access charges over a five-year period, a longer time horizon that will ease the negative effects on labor adjustment. The long-distance lobby (AT&T, MCI, Sprint, and others) had sought complete, immediate reductions. FCC regulators also protected low-end users, raised monthly rates by $1.50 for second lines to residences (e.g., higher-end consumers) and $3.00 for business consumers, and created a special fund to subsidize Internet access to schools and public libraries (Landler 1997).

Meanwhile, at the state level, the ongoing oversight of PUCs constrained the RBOCs' business strategies in ways that directly favored consumers, and indirectly, labor. In the first half of the 1990s, for example, PUCs cited several RBOCs for poor service delivery (Bell Atlantic, NYNEX, and U.S. West), and in some cases (e.g., Bell Atlantic and U.S. West) required the companies to increase staffing levels to meet consumer demands.

State PUCs differ considerably in their standards and policies, and BellSouth and NYNEX represent opposite ends of the spectrum. While NYNEX has historically faced a "tough" New York state utility commission (with respect to rate setting and service standards), BellSouth has faced a more lenient one in its several-state area. BellSouth and NYNEX also operate under distinct labor laws; BellSouth operates almost entirely in "right-to-work" states, with laws that weaken union institutional security. Thus, differences in the political role of the regulators and in labor laws create a distinct institutional framework at the regional level. However, institutional variation does not fully explain the regional variation in restructuring processes and outcomes. In light of weak regional institutional structures for stakeholder participation, the strategic choices of the companies and their unions played a far stronger role in determining the variation of outcomes (Turner 1991).

On the one hand, the BellSouth strategy emphasized joint partnerships to improve customer service, relatively high levels of employment stability (force reductions of roughly 20 percent), but low relative wage and benefit increases. The Communication Workers of America (CWA, of which District 3 represents workers in the BellSouth region) emphasized labor–management cooperation as the most effective way to build union membership and power in the context of weak labor laws. Yet even here, it was difficult to sustain a cooperative approach to implementing work reorganization in the face of anticipated local deregulation. On the other hand, the NYNEX strategy included no union involvement in workplace innovations, high wage and benefit increases, and high levels of workforce reductions (roughly 35–40 percent). The regional union at NYNEX (District 1 of the CWA) had the most militant record of the seven regional districts and pursued the most aggressively adversarial strategy against NYNEX in its six northeastern states. In response, the company sued for labor peace beginning in 1992, a shift in strategy that led to high employment security for the survivor workforce through the most extensive retraining and replacement program in the industry.

BellSouth

Even though BellSouth operates in a relatively weak regulatory environment in right-to-work states, union membership traditionally has been high (over 80 percent of union-eligible employees), and the union and management had adopted a cooperative relationship. This cooperative approach dates to a particularly bitter strike in 1956, after which the company accepted the union as a fact of life and began building a relationship of trust and mutual respect. The union also made the strategic decision to pursue cooperation to keep membership levels high in this right-to-work environment, where workers could choose whether or not to be members and feared management retaliation. Regular interactions between union leadership and management followed the negotiation of a "responsible relationship clause" between AT&T and the CWA in 1966, while by 1971, a problem-solving approach to grievances had reduced the number reaching the state executive level by 50 percent. In 1977 negotiations, the parties agreed to a procedure to expedite arbitrations (Crane 1990).

Experiments in "participatory management" began in the late 1970s (Crane 1990, pp. 34–46), and when AT&T and the national CWA negotiated the joint QWL program in 1980, Southern Bell and CWA District 3 actively implemented it at local worksites. While QWL efforts soon died out in most companies, at BellSouth they still numbered over 600 in 1989 when they were merged into a TQM program. Workers generally viewed QWL programs as a benefit, an example of management actually listening to their concerns. Additionally, the parties at BellSouth developed a joint QWL oversight structure in which management at the district (local), state, and corporate levels invited union leaders to attend regularly scheduled business meetings, an important precedent for subsequent labor–management information sharing and consultation.

In the early 1990s, the parties formalized union participation in monthly business meetings and set up a three-tiered joint structure for union–management collaboration in TQM. The union backed the strategy to improve competitiveness and save jobs. Joint labor–management training teams at the local, state, and corporate levels developed curriculum and provided training to virtually all employees in the company over a two-year period. The trainers also provided technical assistance in problem solving, process improvement, and job redesign efforts such as self-managed teams. The parties also negotiated the parameters for local experimentation in workplace innovations, including telecommuting, self-managed teams, and bringing subcontracted work back in-house.

Local experimentation with TQM and self-managed teams was substantial, and by 1994 both management and the union considered the efforts successful. Twenty percent of workers in network and customer services had participated in TQM problem-solving teams, and 5 percent were participating in self-managed teams. Quantitative evaluation comparing performance of self-managed and traditionally supervised work groups showed significant positive effects of teams for the company, workers, and the union: performance of teams was significantly higher, indirect labor costs fell, workers preferred the arrangements, and nonmanagement jobs were saved at the expense of management jobs (Batt 1999, 2001). A 1996 customer service survey by an independent consulting firm found that BellSouth had the top ratings in customer service of any telephone company (J.D. Power and

Associates 1996). Furthermore, a 1994 survey found that 92 percent of managers and 81 percent of local union presidents supported the union's participation in TQM. Seventy-seven percent of managers and 77 percent of union presidents believed that union participation was critical to the success of TQM. Ninety-seven percent of local union presidents were participating in monthly business meetings, and 32 percent were participating in weekly management staff meetings. Similarly, 90 percent of workers believed the union should participate in TQM, and 60 percent believed union participation was critical to the program's success (Batt 2000b). The union also supported the company in going before state PUCs to gain regulatory reforms that would shift rate regulation from fixed to incentive-based systems, a shift that allowed the company to keep some of its profits from efficiency gains.

The union's participation in partnership strategies depended fundamentally on the company's long-standing commitment to employment and union institutional security and to the mature bargaining relationship that the company and union had achieved. At the time of divestiture, for example, when BellSouth set up a separate subsidiary known as Advanced Systems, Inc. (ASI), it negotiated a separate contract with the CWA rather than operate ASI as a nonunion subsidiary (in contrast to AT&T). In the first round of bargaining after divestiture, BellSouth was the only RBOC to agree to the union's request for regionwide bargaining (as opposed to the more decentralized approach of bargaining with each telephone company in the region). All postdivestiture contracts were approved by the membership without strikes. The company and union also used memoranda of agreement extensively between contracts to promote workplace change. Other negotiated clauses offset the membership declines associated with attrition. A 1989 joint union–management task force studied the content of managerial jobs and returned 550 jobs to the bargaining unit. A 1995 joint study team studied the costs of subcontracting work out and negotiated an agreement to bring the work in-house.

Compared with AT&T and NYNEX, BellSouth has pursued a high relative employment strategy with low relative wages. This strategy may reflect the market characteristics of the region, where (at the time) the population was more rural, geographically dispersed, and growing. Employment fell through attrition by roughly 10,000, or 12 percent of 83,000 employees between 1990 and 1993. Another 10,800 employees were targeted to leave between 1994 and 1996, with roughly equal percentages of managers and workers affected, but many of these proved unnecessary as market conditions improved. Wage increases were relatively low (averaging about 2–3 percent annually after divestiture).

Cooperative labor relations were critical to the considerable experimentation in work innovations at BellSouth. Yet this cooperation was based on the strategic choices of management and labor, rather than through local mandates that would have institutionalized stakeholder participation; and, this cooperative work reorganization occurred in a context in which unilateral management rights threatened to reassert themselves. In fact, by the mid 1990s, BellSouth was adopting a strategy of reengineering, reducing the emphasis on self-managed teams (in spite of their success), and increasing its emphasis on downsizing. This strategic withdrawal from cooperation strained union–management relations, and in 1995 bargaining, the union and management reduced their commitment to joint activities. Management's unilateral decision to focus on reengineering and consolidation of work sites illustrated the weak position of the union in sustaining a cooperative approach in the absence of legal mandates.

NYNEX

In contrast to CWA District 3 at BellSouth, the official position of the regional leadership of both the International Brotherhood of Electrical Workers (IBEW) and the CWA District 1, which represent NYNEX workers, was one of nonparticipation in joint quality and performance-improvement teams. Both unions had a militant history and both continued a traditional approach of "effects bargaining" throughout the 1990s.[8] That is, management makes technology and operational decisions, and the union negotiates the effects of those decisions. Both unions collaborated effectively in a successful three-month strike in 1989 over maintaining health care benefits; they formed a consumer coalition and successfully convinced the New York PUC to refuse the company's request for a rate increase during the strike, a decision that was a major factor in the NYNEX's decision to settle the strike.[9] The unions' militant strategy over the course of the 1980s and early 1990s resulted in the highest wage and benefit increases in the industry. NYNEX negotiated 3–4 percent annual wage increases in all four rounds of bargaining since divestiture in 1984 (almost double those at

BellSouth); it is the only company to continue to provide fully paid health insurance without the requirement of shifting to health maintenance organizations or copayments.

As a result of the 1989 strike, the company made the strategic decision to bring in a seasoned labor relations expert from AT&T (James Dowdall), whose sole purpose was to develop a mature bargaining relationship with the two unions. For 1992 bargaining, Dowdall hosted the unions in a two-week joint training session in mutual gains techniques and paved the way for labor peace. In 1992 bargaining, the company and unions established formal joint committees around technology and workplace issues, but by management and union accounts alike, these existed on paper only. The bitterness evoked during the 1989 strike continued for several years, undermining any real possibility for joint labor–management efforts. Because both unions give considerable autonomy to locals, local union leaders have the choice of participating in joint committees. Only a handful did so, however; the overwhelming majority of local leaders consistently followed district policy, refusing to participate in joint productivity-enhancing programs such as the kind overwhelmingly supported by union leaders at BellSouth. Meanwhile, work restructuring followed a path emphasizing reengineering, the creation of customer service "megacenters," and labor displacement to obtain cost savings.

In spite of their traditionally adversarial bargaining relationship, in 1994 the parties negotiated the most far-reaching employment and union security clauses in the industry. The NYNEX strategy was to build a highly educated, flexible, and productive technical workforce but without employee or union participation in work redesign. In addition to wage increases above the industry average, NYNEX agreed to heavy investment in a two-year training program that created a new multiskilled craft title of "Telecommunications Technical Associate," or "Super-Tech." In the first two years of the program, roughly 1,100 employees enrolled (Clifton 2000). The new contract also developed a force reduction plan with incentives aimed at voluntarily eliminating 16,800 of 57,000 nonmanagement jobs at an estimated cost of over $2 billion, or $77,000 per participating employee (many of these proved unnecessary because market demand increased dramatically). In addition, the contract enabled all NYNEX employees with five years of service to take a two-year educational leave; created a job bank and a new job-sharing provision; guaranteed union workers access to all new NYNEX ventures; ensured that new subsidiaries were required to offer union workers the opportunity to bid into the new jobs; and further enhanced union institutional security through card-check recognition, company neutrality, and access to NYNEX's nonunion workplaces. These provisions helped the CWA win a closely contested union election victory among 1,500 customer service representatives in New England, a unit that had historically been anti-union and had turned down representation in previous campaigns.

In sum, in exchange for high wages, retraining, union security, and expansion into nonunion subsidiaries, the unions agreed to more substantial employment reductions than were taking place at other regional companies, although in the end, these reductions were fewer than expected and occurred through attrition and early retirement buyouts. By 1993, NYNEX had eliminated 19,000 jobs, but only 6,000 were among union members, who accepted generous early retirement offers. The remaining 13,000 were among managers, who either accepted generous settlements or forced layoffs. Under the 1994 contract, the 16,800 nonmanagement jobs targeted for elimination by 1996 would have amounted to an overall drop of at least 35 percent. The company strategy was to build a (smaller) highly skilled, flexible, and productive workforce while maintaining unilateral management rights with respect to operational decision making.

The unions were able to make gains in employment and union institutional security in part because they were able to leverage their power with the state public utility commission. That power was critical to their winning the 1989 strike, which led management to sue for labor peace in the early 1990s. In the 1994 negotiations, management agreed to give the union access to new lines of business in exchange for the union's agreement to support it before the state utility commission. That support was crucial for the company in persuading regulators to allow it to merge with other companies (Bell Atlantic and GTE). Despite these more amicable labor relations, the union and company never experimented with joint workplace innovations. In fact, labor relations deteriorated in the second half of the 1990s as the company experienced unanticipated negative consequences as a result of its downsizing and cost-cutting focus. The demand for data and Internet services and second lines to homes led to an explosion of demand in the latter half of the 1990s. The company substantially underestimated demand growth and overestimated the number of reductions that it needed. In the end, many more employees took the retirement buyouts than the company would have preferred. This change of events created a large understaffing problem, and customer service suffered. The company responded by freezing mobility opportunities for frontline workers and by requiring forced overtime, even for the largely female office workforce that had never had this requirement. These and other conflicts led to a major strike during the 1998 contract negotiations. Thus, the company and unions continue to have very traditional union and management roles, with management retaining decision-making authority and the union engaged in effects bargaining. In contrast to the AT&T case, however, the unions continue to be able to go before state regulators on issues such as adequate staffing for customer service and employment security, to prevent jobs from being outsourced to other states.

GERMANY

The labor-mediated path to a deregulated telecommunications market in Germany has differed substantially from the judicial drive to a free market in the AT&T case as well as the consumer-driven path in the case of the RBOCs. Neocorporatist decision-making structures have resulted in the use of legislation to promote the social market, have created asymmetric structures of regulation which have benefited Deutsche Telekom, and have minimized the negative effects of restructuring on union and employee stakeholders. Consistent with the promotion of the social market, stakeholders (including the firm, employees, unions, suppliers, and to some extent residential consumers) have been full participants in restructuring at both the industry and firm level, influencing the speed, form, and structure of the reregulated product market, and developing new work practices, labor adjustment, and corporate structures. However, once European Union (EU) policies began to drive deregulation, they helped undermine the influence of stakeholders and actually altered the nature of Germany's semisovereign state (Darbishire 1997b, 2000; Katzenstein 1987).

In perpetuating the social market, the participation of multiple stakeholders in a quasi-corporatist policymaking process has resulted in a path of restructuring that exhibits high levels of stability, limited deregulation, and limited labor displacement. In contrast to the United States, a strategy of technological displacement of labor and cost minimization has not dominated. Of equal importance, however, the performance of Telekom has continued to lag behind that of AT&T and the RBOCs along several dimensions: slower restructuring to take advantage of new technology, difficulty in reorienting Telekom from providing a basic social infrastructure to being a critical input into business competitiveness, and fewer experiments or innovations in work organization. The costs of restructuring also have been distributed significantly differently among the stakeholders, with customers receiving poorer service and higher costs.

In spite of being highly competent technologically and having the largest cable TV and integrated services digital network (ISDN) in the world, Deutsche Telekom has been slow to utilize the potential of new technology. By 1994, for example, only 30 percent of network switching and transmission was digital, compared with 100 percent in the United States and Britain. The availability of services from Telekom has also been poor, and problems include underdevelopment of data transmission, absence of itemized billing, high prices, long waiting lists for installation and repair, and high fault rates (DTI 1994). The lack of integrated computer systems to provide enhanced customer service has compounded these problems, while organizational and network structures and operating procedures have been slow to adjust and realize performance gains, even where new technology has been introduced. Furthermore, slow digitalization of the network and poor performance occurred in spite of Telekom investing substantially more than other telecommunications companies in the 1980s (Gerpott and Pospischil 1993; Darbishire 1997a).

In parallel with the United States, the telecommunications market in Germany historically was organized as a closely regulated monopoly. However, it also operated under public ownership and, until 1989, as part of the Deutsche Bundespost jointly with the postal and telegraph services. As part of the Ministry of Posts and Telecommunications, regulatory and operational decision making were not separated, and Telekom was immediately subordinate to the federal minister.

With an underlying mandate of public service comparable to that of AT&T prior to divestiture, Telekom focused on its public service obligations and underplayed commercial objectives. Similarly, Telekom's universal focus meant that it was slow to respond to the capabilities of new technologies and use them to develop differentiated market segments or meet the divergent demands of business and residential customers.

Repeated attempts to reform the Deutsche Bundespost in the 1960s and 1970s included proposals to create a management structure with greater independence from political influence and to operate Telekom on business principles. Although reform proposals clearly accepted the principle that public ownership, monopoly provision, universal service, and social welfare obligations should be retained, these attempts failed, largely because of union opposition (Duch 1991; Noam 1992).

In 1982 the Bundespost as a whole was responsible for 3.4 percent of the German gross national product (GNP), contributed 10 percent of its revenues to the government, employed 500,000 workers, and was by far the most important purchaser of equipment from Siemens, one of the world's largest telecommunications equipment manufacturers (Noam 1992). However, this is insufficient to explain Deutsche Telekom's slow process of deregulation, because AT&T was in a similar position as the world's largest company, with over one million employees. Rather, in contrast to the United States, German unions succeeded in watering down policy initiatives during the 1980s. German institutional structures grant social partners, such as the unions, a substantially greater institutionalized voice in the management of the economy, and in the structure and timing of deregulation, than does the United States. This neocorporatist role of the social partners, a central component of what Katzenstein (1987) characterizes as the "semisovereign state," substantially limits the extent of deregulation.

The neocorporatist structures allowed the stakeholders (employees, unions, and their work councils) within the Bundespost to form a passive coalition against any fundamental shift in the strategic orientation (or organization) of the telecommunications industry, such as implied by digitalization. In contrast to the United States, no dominant reformist business cohort could form in Germany to promote a significant deregulation of the industry, in large part because of the institutionalized position of existing stakeholders. The stakeholders included not only employees, but also suppliers, who long operated an effective cartel in the equipment market, with prices substantially above world levels (Darbishire 1997b).

The continued debate over the structure of the Deutsche Bundespost and, as importantly, over the inaction that resulted from each reform attempt, was reflected in the influential 1987 report of the Witte Commission. This body was appointed by the government to examine the future structure of the telecommunications industry. The Commission reflected neocorporatism in Germany, as well as the institutionalization of stakeholders' voice, and took one year to establish because the panel needed to include not only all four major political parties but also the unions, Bundespost officials, and business (though there were no representatives of users on the Commission). The inclusion of a broad range of stakeholders ensured that a moderate compromise resulted.

The report recommended separating the entrepreneurial functions of telecommunications management from regulatory decisions; increasing managerial independence; separating the three Bundespost companies (post, bank, and telecommunications); bringing prices increasingly in line with costs and focusing more on profits; and increasing the flexibility of the companies in personnel policy (Witte 1987). After a series of debates over the Witte recommendations, the government implemented these changes under Post Reform I (July 1, 1989), and also introduced elements of competition into the terminal equipment, value-added network services, and mobile telecommunications markets. The Deutsche Postgewerkschaft (DPG) union consistently opposed these changes, though the ability to block change is less a feature of corporatism than the ability to significantly influence policy. Thus, the compromise nature of Post Reform I ensured that Telekom retained its critical monopoly over telephony services and the network itself, which constituted 90 percent of its revenue.

The debates surrounding Post Reform I contrasted significantly with those in the United States over deregulation. In particular, the structure of the reregulated product market was not determined by "secondary" actors (such as the courts) but importantly by those stakeholders most critically affected by deregulation, including employees, unions, and the company itself. The endogeneity of decision making was characteristic of neocorporatism, a key feature of the German model, which applies particularly to corporate bodies such as the Bundespost, which were founded under public law to carry out important policy functions. The unions were in a position to substantively affect both the timing and extent of regulatory change. Indeed, with respect to telecommunications policy, "all the way up to the Federal Chancellor there are people who want to avoid a conflict with the DPG [Deutsche Postgewerkschaft]," given the strength of the union's influence (Morgan and Webber 1986, p. 69). The vigorous opposition of the DPG to any change in the structure of the Bundespost, or to that of the telecommunications market, reflected its concerns about the impact of new technology. In particular, the DPG was concerned that the new technology would allow cost cutting through employment reductions. The union also was concerned that liberalization threatened a significant decline in its role, which had long been one of the strongest and most influential in Germany.

Pressure to further restructure Telekom resurfaced far more rapidly than had been anticipated after Post Reform I. The privatization of Telekom under Post Reform II was enacted in 1994 and driven by three factors. First, pressure from the EU played an increasing role in determining the pace of deregulation. The European Commission issued a series of directives under Article 90 of the Treaty of Rome, which successfully forced the majority of EU countries, including Germany, to agree to open their telephony services market by 1998. Because the effect of EU policies was to increasingly dictate the regulatory structure and enforce competition, the very nature of debates within Germany was narrowed. Consequently, Post Reform II did not even address deregulation but rather confined itself to privatization. The central focus of Post Reform I debates, therefore, was removed from the arena, and German stakeholders could have little influence on it. Furthermore, EU directives on procurement policies undermined the possibility of member states having national champion equipment suppliers, and consequently meant that companies such as Siemens had progressively less interest in maintaining the status quo.

Second, and also of considerable importance, German unification resulted in the need for Telekom to undertake a massive upgrading of the east German network, with a projected cost of DM 60 billion between 1990 and 1997. Given increasing budgetary pressures, the government proposed the privatization of Telekom under Post Reform

II to help fund unification. Because Telekom itself had a deteriorating financial position, reflected in a declining reserve asset ratio,[10] Telekom management and political parties regarded privatization as a necessary step to rectify this weakness. Third, given the growing importance of the international telecommunications market and an increasing emphasis on international joint ventures, Telekom management promoted privatization to remove restrictions from Telekom's global ambitions. Furthermore, the inevitability of product market deregulation led Telekom to argue that it needed to be released from the political control and bureaucracy of the public sector (Darbishire 1995).

In addition to generating greater stability in the telecommunications market in Germany, the integrated role of key stakeholders, particularly employees and unions, helped them protect their own interests. The DPG principally campaigned for employee and union institutional security. At the industry level, both the *Länder,* or federal states, and the DPG were concerned with how EU policies to liberalize the product market would be enacted in Germany. Stakeholders ensured their influence on the structure of the product market through the creation of a Regulatory Council under Post Reform II restructuring. Through this council, for example, they ensured the adoption of a high standard of universal service (of general ISDN availability) by the end of 1995. By establishing the general availability of a high level of service as a matter of public policy, stakeholders had substantially greater input into the product market structure than in the United States, while simultaneously constraining the strategic options available to Telekom.

During the political negotiations over Post Reform II, the DPG secured the right to bargain with Telekom in all of its subsidiaries, which were in turn bound to negotiate with the DPG. Through this mechanism, the DPG constrained Telekom from even considering a nonunion employment strategy (Darbishire 1997a). Employee representation on the Supervisory Board was made uniquely strong, even in a German context, while employee concerns about the postprivatization structure of works councils led to additional alterations. These included the initial extension of the three-tier, public-sector works council structure to the privatized Telekom, as well as a higher number of works councilors (Darbishire 1995). Furthermore, the DPG secured the continuation of the contractual rights of all its employees, including their impressive employment security guarantees (which apply to civil servants, who constitute half of Telekom's workforce, as well as to all workers aged 40, with 15 years of service). These rights have, in turn, constrained Telekom from adopting a technological displacement strategy and substantially downsizing its workforce.

The institutional constraints on Telekom's labor market approach are illustrated by the relative employment stability within the company. Between 1984 and 1994, Telekom employment in West Germany was virtually unchanged, with a decrease of only 4,000 from 191,000. Total employment, including the former East German telephone workers, stood at 225,435. It was only in March 1995 that Telekom officially doubled its goal of eliminating 30,000 jobs throughout East and West Germany to 60,000 (26 percent of the workforce) by the year 2000.

While the extent of potential technological displacement should not be underestimated, Telekom's underlying strategy has emphasized a revenue-enhancing, up-market approach, with slow, heavily negotiated change. The emphasis on revenue generation rather than technological displacement, downsizing, or cost minimization is significant. In contrast to the United States, where access lines per employee is the standard performance measure, Telekom established a corporate objective of revenue per employee, set at DM 470,000. This measure has underlain Telekom's strategy, substantially promoted by the DPG, of seeking new employment opportunities rather than cutting costs. By mid 1995, the DPG presented Telekom with over 50 proposals of how to generate new business to enhance employment security. Telekom took these proposals seriously, especially because of the downsizing constraints it faced because the DPG had made employment security its top priority.

The rights of the works councils—concerning the introduction of new technology and restructuring of work, and the regrading of employees, transfers, and appointments—required that Telekom work cooperatively with the union. For example, between June 1993 and March 1994, the DPG negotiated a unique contract in response to the proposed elimination of 11,000 posts under a restructuring program known as Telekom Service 2000. This contract guaranteed employment security to all workers affected by restructuring and specified compensation for those adversely affected by the cost-cutting plan. In late 1994, the DPG extended this contract (in negotiations over a broader reorganization plan) to all workers, thereby guaranteeing comprehensive employment security until the end of June 1996. Moreover, Telekom's plan to downsize by 60,000 was premised on the use of expensive voluntary redundancy and early retirement packages.

The positive impact of these industrial relations on Telekom's business strategy was facilitated by the favorable regulatory environment that Telekom enjoyed and the absence of countervailing financial market pressures. Rather than being constrained by asymmetric regulatory structures from entering closely aligned market segments (as, for example, AT&T was in the local market and the RBOCs were in the cable TV market), Telekom continued to operate the largest cable TV company in the world with a *de facto* monopoly and had 14.6 million subscribers by the end of 1994. Combined with the largest ISDN network, these conditions provided Telekom with the potential for the development of an integrated telecommunications services industry and an up-market strategy generating new, high-quality businesses.

However, despite longer time horizons, a favorable regulatory climate, and the integration of DPG and works councils into decision making, Telekom has continued to be slow in developing innovative work practices or effective restructuring. For example, management viewed the lack of local autonomy as a principal deficit of its organizational structure and a division of the corporate structure needed to meet differentiated customer demands. Telekom initiated a project in 1993–1994 to reorganize the company into three decentralized divisions (serving business and residential customers, and managing the network). Although this model drew on successful U.S. and U.K. experience and involved substantial works council and union participation at every stage, the reform proceeded in a slow, cautious, and centralized manner. This project included testing two competing models of corporate structure. One, favored by Telekom management, was based principally on market segments and another (favored by the DPG) on geographic units (Darbishire 1997a). The piloting of competing models indicates the strength of the union's influence in seeking to minimize the perceived negative effect of restructuring on union and worker interests.

Unlike the slow pace of corporate restructuring, digitalization of the network has led to substantial work reorganization and operational cost cutting. As in the United States, this change involved a shift away from functional organization, though significantly without any attempt to increase the extent of Taylorism or machine pacing of work, as at AT&T and the RBOCs. Rather, digitalization occurred in the context of intensive consultation and agreements with the central works council, which utilized its codetermination rights to ensure that systems capable of monitoring workers' behavior have neither been used to do that nor to intensify the pace of work.

In summary, rather than adopting a cost-minimization or labor-intensification strategy, Telekom instead fully involved works councils and the union in the process of restructuring. As a result, it did not experience the declines in morale or cooperative union–management activity experienced in the United States. Nevertheless, there have been no decentralized workplace trials equivalent to those in the United States. Three factors contributed to this outcome. First, Telekom was slow to decentralize its operational structures, characteristic of its public sector legacy. This tardiness restricted its potential for workplace innovation. Second, the union and works councils were strongly focused on the technological displacement and downsizing implications of restructuring. Third, because employee representatives feared that restructuring had the potential to undermine their position, they attempted to minimize its downside by conducting highly detailed, centralized negotiations about new work organization practices.

More generally, the restricted pattern of workplace innovation reflects the radical nature of technological change in the telecommunications industry. Although extensive worker and works council involvement have promoted such innovation in industries experiencing incremental changes in technology, in the telecommunications industry the situation differs. Workers perceive that technical changes will undermine their existing skill sets as jobs become based more on knowledge of software, clerical, and service skills. Potential gains from the transformation of work in the telecommunications industry derive from new skill sets and cross-functional organizational integration as described in the AT&T and RBOC sections, not from building on these workers' existing craft skills (Darbishire 1997b; Lehrer and Darbishire 1997). The combination of strong worker rights, together with a negative perception of the adjustment process, led to a more cautious restructuring of Telekom's product market, although it generated a significantly different outcome in the labor market.

CONCLUSION

What lessons for mutual learning can be gained from these comparisons? Several are noteworthy. At the most basic level, the ability of stakeholders to influence or control the pace of change significantly affects the outcomes. The weak institutional position of unions in the AT&T case prevented them from slowing the course of change. The unions in the regional Bell cases did not have more power but could leverage concern for consumer welfare to slow the pace of change. By contrast, the institutional power of the German unions allowed them to significantly slow the pace to explicitly address labor's concerns.

The slower pace of restructuring in both the regional Bell and Telekom cases provided a longer time horizon to develop a range of labor adjustment strategies to meet the needs of both management and labor. At a minimum, these strategies included softening the negative effect on the displaced workforce through the use of attrition, voluntary severance, and early retirement programs. These strategies also had positive "spillover" effects on the morale of the survivor workforce. For management, this positive effect on morale increased the likelihood that the survivor workforce would play a more cooperative role in ongoing restructuring. Additionally, the longer time horizon provided the needed time for retraining and redeployment, strategies that benefited not only the incumbent workforce but management as well by building on the embedded skill base rather than losing that base to competitors.

By contrast, the faster, unconstrained approach allowed companies to take advantage of the full implications of new technology and market flexibility, both in terms of process and product innovation. In the United States, the most significant outcome of this decade of market-driven restructuring has been to alter the fundamental purpose of the telecommunications industry. Its mission has changed from providing an integrated universal service to the public and maintaining national security to supporting national economic competitiveness in a global economy. In general, then, the U.S. telecommunications industry has outperformed its German counterpart in terms of speed of delivery, response time, product diversity, and price reductions—both as an input into other industries and as a direct contributor to national economic growth. However, employees bore the major costs of restructuring through displacement, decline in morale, and ongoing employment insecurity. Labor market segmentation increased. Unions lost power and members.

In Germany, by contrast, the influence of government policymakers, unions, and corporate stakeholders in slowing the pace of restructuring prevented Telekom from taking advantage of the implications of new technologies, limiting performance improvements for business and residential consumers. However, workers have not suffered the kind of displacement, demoralization, or insecurity that U.S. workers have faced. Unions have retained membership levels as well as their institutional power.

These findings would argue for a classic story of the trade-offs between consumer and worker welfare. While in the short run, this argument has some merit, the longer-term outcomes are far from certain. First, to the extent that rapid, market-driven deregulation leads to efficiency and innovation, corporate users and the national economy more generally benefit. Certainly, the United States continues to lead the world in innovations in telecommunications technologies. But it is difficult to ascribe this positive outcome entirely to deregulation, because the United States historically led the world in this field (Vietor 1989; Rosenberg 1994).

Second, haste makes waste. AT&T's divestiture and deregulation were premised on the assumption that new microwave technologies would erode the natural monopoly argument in the telecommunications market. However, the digitalization of network switching and transmission systems substantially increased network economies of scale and scope. This has led some who are strongly pro-deregulation to admit that technological efficiencies may lead to a recentralization of the industry (Huber 1989). The 1990s have confirmed some of these worries, as merger activity has dominated the decade, exemplified by the eight large local carriers at divestiture (the seven RBOCs and GTE) that have merged into four. In addition, some researchers have argued that significant reductions in productivity growth have accompanied this period of duplication and overcapacity. Using three different measures of productivity used in the industry,[11] Keefe found that productivity growth in the 1984–1991 period (3.4 percent annually) was half that of the 1974–1983 period (6.9 percent per year) and the 1951–1983 period (6 percent per year). By the early 1990s, when AT&T served 60 percent of the long-distance market, MCI and Sprint together had the capacity to meet the needs of the entire country (Keefe and Boroff 1994, pp. 321–322). Moreover, while corporations benefited from competition in the equipment industry, the U.S. economy suffered as imports rose dramatically (from Canada's Northern Telecom and Germany's Siemens). U.S. manufacturers of telecommunications equipment were decimated.

Third, the distribution of benefits to consumers in the United States has been highly unequal. Large business users have benefited the most. Small business and residential consumers have also benefited through greater product diversity and reductions in the price of long distance, which offset price increases in basic service. Notably, however, residential consumers were protected because regulators slowed the pace of deregulation in local service. Otherwise, basic rates would have skyrocketed in the 1980s. Low-end consumers fared worse under deregulation in the 1980s and 1990s because basic rates rose and they could not afford to take advantage of long-distance price reductions. While new FCC regulations seek to ensure universal service as well as Internet access to low-income residents, the implementation of regulations will determine longer-term outcomes.

It is not only pace of change that matters, however. As we have argued, more fundamentally, the outcomes depend on the relative power and strategic choices of institutional actors and stakeholders in shaping the trajectory of deregulation and restructuring. In the AT&T case, the courts and regulators deliberately chose to reduce the profitability of AT&T, and the company, unions, and consumers were excluded from the decision-making process. In the case of the regional Bells, political embeddedness gave the companies, unions, and residential consumers a position to win politically favorable legislation that tempered a free-market approach. In the German case, institutional stakeholders deliberately chose an approach to reregulation that privileges Telekom by retaining its monopoly in telephony and cable TV. This choice provided the opportunity for a carefully managed, integrated approach to restructuring and the provision of multimedia services. Although the EU may alter its adjustment path, Germany has the potential to avoid duplicating its infrastructure as did the United States, where the systemness of technology continues to favor economies of scale. The German social market solution has the potential in the long run to create mutual gains for firms, unions, employees, and consumers. Yet the promise is still to be fulfilled.

Finally, it is noteworthy that none of the approaches to reregulation and restructuring has achieved a new system of "high-involvement" work organization comparable to the innovative team-based or lean production systems in manufacturing. While more experimentation has occurred in the United States, those experiments have been short-lived, overcome by broad-scale cost-cutting initiatives. Meanwhile, Telekom and the German unions have positioned themselves for greater labor–management cooperation in workplace innovations. Rather than adopting a cost minimization or technological displacement strategy, Telekom has focused on a revenue enhancement strategy. This has the potential to create a high-involvement approach to work organization while limiting the ultimate costs and adjustment burden borne by employees and the union. Of key importance, however, is whether the cautious but sustained cooperative approach to restructuring will produce performance gains in the long run. The outcome will itself be strongly influenced by the ability of stakeholders to successfully implement changes to sustain the up-market strategy in spite of ongoing downsizing and before new competitive entrants can erode Telekom's substantial market share.

Notes

1. Until 1984, AT&T, or the "Bell system," was a regulated monopoly composed of Bell Labs (the research and development arm); Western Electric (the equipment-producing arm); AT&T long lines (the long-distance arms), and 22 local Bell companies (the local service providers). In response to a lawsuit filed by MCI, which sought entry into AT&T markets, the courts dismantled the monopoly. AT&T retained ownership of the equipment and long-distance subsidiaries but not local service. The 22 local phone companies were reorganized into seven regional Bell operating companies (RBOCs) with monopoly control of local service; they also jointly owned Bell Labs until 1996.
2. Source: author's interviews with Bell company representatives.

3. NYNEX comprises the New York and New England telephone companies. It merged with Bell Atlantic, which subsequently merged with GTE to form Verizon. In this chapter, we refer to the company as NYNEX because the material is specific to NYNEX before it merged with Bell Atlantic.
4. AT&T unsuccessfully led a coalition of consumers, unions, independent telephone companies, and state PUCs.
5. *Taylorism*, after Frederick Taylor, refers to the practice of using time and motion studies to separate thought from execution and break down complex jobs into narrow repetitive tasks to improve efficiency.
6. Source: author's interviews with management and union officials.
7. Moreover, heightened transaction costs and consumer confusion, for example, are a consequence of the package deals to consumers (such as MCI's Friends and Family and AT&T's Reach Out and True Voice). This trend is in sharp contrast to current theories of quality in customer service that argue that customer loyalty and longevity are the key to competitiveness (Schlesinger and Heskett 1991a, 1991b).
8. A 1996 union election replaced the long-standing CWA district leadership with a leadership team more open to joint strategies, but the company was focused on merger activity (with Bell Atlantic and GTE). Contract negotiations in 1998 and 2001 were settled only after a strike.
9. For a fuller account of the unions' use of the state utility commission to curb corporate behavior, see Katz, Batt, and Keefe (2000).
10. Having amounted to 30 percent in 1990 and 25 percent in 1992, the reserve asset ratio was projected to fall to 18 percent by 1994.
11. These measures are average annual increases in access lines per employee hour, in switched minutes per employee hour, and in adjusted revenue per employee hour.

References

Aronson, Jonathan, and Peter Cowhey. 1988. *When Countries Talk: International Trade in Telecommunications Services*. Lexington, Massachusetts: American Enterprise Institute/Ballinger.

Batt, Rosemary. 1999. "Work Organization, Technology, and Performance in Customer Service and Sales." *Industrial and Labor Relations Review* 52(4): 539–564.

_____. 2000a. "Strategic Segmentation and Frontline Services: Matching Customers, Employees, and Human Resource Systems." *International Journal of Human Resource Management* 11(3): 540–562.

_____. 2000b. "When Do Employees Benefit from Teams and Why?" Unpublished manuscript.

_____. 2001. "The Economics of Teams among Technicians." *British Journal of Industrial Relations* 39(1): 1–24.

Batt, Rosemary, and Jeffrey Keefe. 1999. "Human Resource and Employment Practices in Telecommunications Services." In *Employment Practices and Business Strategy,* Peter Cappelli, ed. Oxford: Oxford University
Press, pp. 107–152.

Batt, Rosemary, and Michael Strausser. 1998. "Labor Market Outcomes of
Deregulation in Telecommunications Services." *Proceedings of the 50th
Annual Meetings of the IRRA.* Madison, Wisconsin: IRRA Series

Clifton, Jean. 2000. "Restructuring the Employment Relationship: Implications for Firms, Unions, and Employees." Ph.D. dissertation, School of
Industrial and Labor Relations, Cornell University.

Cohen, Jeffrey. 1992. *The Politics of Telecommunications Regulation: The
States and the Divestiture of AT&T.* Armonk, New York: M.E. Sharpe
Publishing.

Coll, Steve. 1986. *The Deal of the Century: The Breakup of AT&T.* New
York: Atheneum Press.

Crane, Donald. 1990. *Patterns of Industrial Peace: Case Studies of Cooperative, Collective Bargaining Relationships.* Research Monograph no. 102.
Atlanta: Georgia State University Business Press.

Darbishire, Owen. 1995. "Switching Systems: Technological Change, Competition, and Privatisation." *Industrielle Bezihungen* 2(2): 156–179.

_____. 1997a. "Germany." In *Telecommunications: Restructuring Work
and Employment Relations Worldwide,* Harry Katz, ed. Ithaca, New York:
ILR Press, Cornell University.

_____. 1997b. "Radical versus Incremental Restructuring: Employment
Relations in the Telecommunications Industry." Working paper, Pembroke
College, University of Oxford.

_____. Forthcoming. "Transforming Telecommunications: Institutional and
Stakeholder Impacts on Strategy, Work Restructuring and Employment
Relations." Ph.D. dissertation, Cornell University.

DTI. 1994. *Study of the International Competitiveness of the UK Telecommunications Infrastructure.* Robert Harrison, PA Consulting Group, Department of Trade and Industry of the U.K.

Duch, Raymond M. 1991. *Privatizing the Economy: Telecommunications
Policy in Comparative Perspective.* Ann Arbor: University of Michigan
Press.

FCC. 1992/1993. *Statistics of Communications Common Carriers.* Federal
Communications Commission, Washington, D.C.: U.S. Government Print-
ing Office.

Gerpott, Torsten J., and Rudolf Pospischil. 1993. "Internationale Effizienz-
vergleiche der DBP Telekom: Ergebnisse eines Benchmarking-Projektes
zur Unterstützung von organisatorischem Wandel in einem staatlichen

Telekommunikationsunternehmen" (International Efficiency Comparisons of the DBP Telekom: Results of a Benchmarking Project in Support of Organizational Change in a National Telecommunications Enterprise). *Zeitschift für betriebswirtschaftliche Forschung* 4: 366–389.

Huber, Peter. 1989. "The Technological Imperative for Competition." In *Future Competition in Telecommunications*, Stephen Bradley and Jerry Hausman, eds. Boston: Harvard Business School Press, pp. 105–122.

J.D. Power and Associates. 1996. *Study of Residential Local Telephone Companies*. Photocopy, J.D. Power and Associates, Agoura Hills, California.

Katz, Harry, ed. 1997. *Telecommunications: Restructuring Work and Employment Relations Worldwide*. Ithaca, New York: ILR Press, Cornell University.

Katz, Harry, Rosemary Batt, and Jeffrey Keefe. 2000. "The Strategic Initiatives of the CWA: Organizing, Politics, and Collective Bargaining." Unpublished manuscript.

Katzenstein, Peter J. 1987. *Policy and Politics in West Germany: The Growth of a Semisovereign State*. Philadelphia: Temple University Press.

Keefe, Jeffrey, and Rosemary Batt. 1997. "United States." In *Telecommunications: Restructuring Work and Employment Relations Worldwide*, Harry Katz, ed. Ithaca, New York: ILR Press, Cornell University, pp. 31–58.

Keefe, Jeffrey, and Karen Boroff. 1994. "Telecommunications Labor Management Relations after Divestiture." In *Contemporary Collective Bargaining in the Private Sector*, Paula Voos, ed. Madison, Wisconsin: Industrial Relations Research Association, pp. 303–372.

Landler, Mark. 1997. "Big Restructuring of Phone Charges Approved by F.C.C." *The New York Times* (May 8), p. 1.

Lehrer, Mark, and Owen Darbishire. 1997. "The Performance of Economic Institutions in a Dynamic Environment: Air Transport and Telecommunications in Germany and Britain (summary in German)." Working paper FS I 97-301, Wissenschaftzentrum, Berlin, Germany, pp. 97–301.

MacDuffie, John Paul, and Michael Maccoby. 1986. "The Organizational Implications of New Technologies: Remote Work Centers at AT&T Communications." Discussion paper, JFK School of Government, Harvard University, Cambridge, Massachusetts.

Morgan, Kevin, and Douglas Webber. 1986. "Divergent Paths: Political Strategies for Telecommunications in Britain, France and West Germany." In *The Politics of the Communications Revolution in Western Europe,* Kenneth Dyson and Peter Humphreys, eds. London: Frank Cass Publisher.

Noam, Eli. 1992. *Telecommunications in Europe*. Oxford: Oxford University Press.

Rosenberg, Nathan. 1994. "Telecommunications: Complex, Uncertain, and Path Dependent." In *Exploring the Black Box: Technology, Economics, and History.* Cambridge: Cambridge University Press, pp. 203–231.

Schlesinger, Leonard, and James Heskett. 1991a. "Breaking the Cycle of Failure in Services." *Sloan Management Review* 32(Spring): 17–28.

_____. 1991b. "The Service-Driven Company." *Harvard Business Review* 69(Sept./Oct.): 73–81.

Stone, Alan. 1989. *Wrong Number: The Breakup of AT&T.* New York: Basic Books.

Temin, Peter. 1987. *The Fall of the Bell System: A Study in Prices and Politics.* Cambridge: Cambridge University Press.

Teske, Paul. 1990. *After Divestiture: The Political Economy of State Telecommunications Regulation.* SUNY Series in Public Administration. Albany, New York: State University of New York Press.

Turner, Lowell. 1991. *Democracy at Work: Changing World Markets and the Future of Labor Unions.* Ithaca, New York: Cornell University Press.

Vietor, Richard. 1989. "AT&T and the Public Good: Regulation and Competition in Telecommunications, 1910–1987." In *Future Competition in Telecommunications*, Stephen P. Bradley and Jerry A. Hausman, eds. Boston: Harvard Business School Press, pp. 27–103.

Witte, Eberhard. 1987. *Neuordnung der Telekommunikation: Bericht der Regierungskommission Fernmeldewesen.* Heidelberg, Germany: G. Schenck.

3

Institutional Effects on Skill Creation and Management Development in the United States and Germany

David Finegold
University of Southern California

Brent Keltner
Englishexchange.com

Political economists are devoting greater attention to issues of skill development and corporate restructuring (Streeck 1989; Finegold and Soskice 1988). The shift from a focus on inflation and the welfare state to education, training, and economic competitiveness reflects the profound shifts that have taken place in the global economy in the last decade. The combination of the growing interdependence of national economies, the emergence of new, low-cost but relatively high-quality competitors, and rapid technological change has led many to conclude that the only way for the advanced industrial countries to maintain or improve their standard of living is to raise the skill levels of their citizens (Reich 1991). Likewise, education and training are seen as one of the main solutions to the growth in wage inequality that characterized many of the developed economies in the 1980s and early 1990s (OECD 1994).

Most of the comparative work by new institutionalists on skill issues has focused on the relative success of different national or regional vocational education and training systems in producing craft and technical skills (e.g., Ryan 1991; Finegold and Mason 1996). These intermediate skills are seen as an essential component for introducing flexible production regimes (e.g., Streeck 1989; Finegold and Wagner 1997). Interestingly, there has been relatively little comparative institutional research on the skills of the individuals responsible for designing and implementing workplace restructuring, i.e., company managers. This chapter is an attempt to start filling that gap, focusing on how national institutional structures shape different models of management development in the United States and Germany. It compares and contrasts the roles of the state, intermediary institutions, the market, and firms in each setting in developing managerial skills.

We adopted a broad definition of *management development* for the study. By *manager* we mean any individual who oversees other employees, from frontline supervisors to chief executives, while *skill development* includes activities beyond formal education and training, such as planned job rotation. Our focus is thus broader than most previous comparative studies of management development, which have tended to confine themselves to top managers and the university programs they attend (e.g., Commonwealth of Australia 1982; Handy 1987). For example, we include the major contribution that two-year colleges and firm-based training make to management development in our analysis.

We conducted semistructured interviews with the main providers of management development in each nation: education and training institutions (both public and private) and companies. For the companies in each country, we identified a sample that met the following criteria: 1) participates in the global economy (including through exports or servicing international customers; 2) is a mixture of large and small (fewer than 100 employees) operations; 3) represents best practices in management development (as identified by peers or our review of the management literature); 4) represents one of three manufacturing (food processing, precision engineering, and electronics) or three service (hotels, banks, and business services) sector enterprises. We also interviewed relevant professional organizations, policymakers, and experts in management development.

Within each organization, we tried to interview more than one individual to get different perspectives (i.e., human resource and production managers, professors, and deans) on the issues of management development. In all, we conducted 50 interviews in the United States (29 with education providers and 21 with company managers) and 39 interviews in Germany (21 with education providers and management experts and 18 with firm managers). We supplemented the interviews with reviews of the relevant literature and the national and international data available on management development.

Our interviews confirmed that major changes under way in the world economy—increased competition, globalization, pressures for customization and enhanced quality, technological change, and shifts toward flatter, more team-based organizations—are forcing institutions involved in management development in both countries to develop a broad range of new capabilities for their management workforce (e.g., Lawler 1996). At the same time, however, managers continue to need strong technical and interpersonal skills to help them act as organizational leaders. Chief among the new demands is the need to combine analytic and interpersonal skills earlier in a manager's career. With firms reducing management layers and relying more on teams to customize output, a growing number of managers need both "hard" and "soft" skills right from the outset if they are to function effectively. Among these soft skills, firms in both countries are placing a growing emphasis on interpersonal management skills, such as the ability to facilitate group work.

A second new skill demand is the capacity of managers to become effective lifelong learners. As companies remove layers from managerial hierarchies, more managers face career paths that are horizontal across a number of different functions in the organization or across several companies, rather than a more vertical ("stovepiped") progression within a single field of expertise (Kiechel 1994). To cope with this uncertain environment, managers need both a broad initial education and continuing opportunities to update or alter their skills. As one American woman who had successfully progressed from a clerical worker to a middle manager while acquiring two degrees part time put it: "What you really need is your own personal career counselor. But since the company isn't going to provide that, you need to take ownership over your own career development." In addition, managers need to develop the capabilities to learn from different experiences, a set of attributes that recent research has shown to be a strong predictor of successful international executives (Spreitzer, McCall, and Mahoney 1997).

A third related emerging skill need is that of developing global capabilities. With the continued internationalization of all aspects of the world economy (goods and services, information, capital and labor), both organizations and individuals need to enhance their ability to operate effectively across national, institutional, and cultural boundaries (Finegold 1997). Firms need managers who can coordinate design and production on a worldwide basis (Sabbagh 1996) as well as establish new markets in other nations and lead or participate effectively in transnational teams (Snow, Snell, and Davison 1996).

Our study focused on the different institutional arrangements for management development in the United States and Germany and how well they are coping with these new demands. To summarize our main findings, the strengths and weaknesses of the two countries' systems in preparing managers for both traditional and emerging skill needs are essentially mirror images of each other. Germany's strong employer organizations and quasi-public institutions have contributed to broad initial skill development and strong technical skills, but the overregulation and heavy dependence of universities on state funding has discouraged the innovation in management education needed to keep apace of the international shifts in the global economy. The organization of skill development within firms, moreover, has made it difficult to develop many managers' cross-functional skills. In contrast, intense competition among public and private business schools in the United States has produced global leadership in graduate management education and research. Also, the flexible internal structures of leading U.S. corporations have enabled them to adapt training programs to more decentralized, leaner organizations by promoting cross-functional skills among all managers. The reliance on the market, however, has led to greater variation in the quality and quantity of technical and organizational training for supervisors and managers in small firms. Some states are experimenting with creative new institutional arrangements for developing the capabilities of individuals and smaller firms that otherwise do not invest heavily in management training.

CONCEPTUAL FRAMEWORK

Four main types of institutional arrangements govern economic activity generally and the development of managerial skills in particular: the market, internal firm hierarchies, intermediate organizations (such as employer associations) and the state (see Hollingsworth, Schmitter, and Streeck 1994; Crouch, Finegold, and Sako, 1999). All countries will have a mix of these different institutional mechanisms, or what we call "models of management development." How effective each combination of models is in the United States and Germany depends, to a large extent, on the fit between the kinds of skills required and the type of model being used to develop them.

Human capital theory suggests that the market should produce an optimum level of skill investment. The theory has traditionally distinguished between two types of skills, general and firm-specific (Becker 1975). General skills, which can be transferred easily from one firm to another, will (according to the theory) be financed by individuals who can then recoup the investment through higher wages. Many managerial competencies fall into this category, for example, good communication skills, problem-solving abilities, and leadership. Because there is a high private rate of return to those who possess these competencies (Finegold and Brewer 1996), individuals should be willing to undertake and finance education or training experiences that help develop these skills.

Firms will, along with their employees, cover the costs of developing skills that are specific to their enterprise, such as an understanding of a particular corporate culture or mastery of a set of internal practices required for the organization to operate effectively. Unlike the predictions of human capital theory, however, which treat the firm as a black box, institutional and management research shows that there are significant differences in the structure of firms among countries, and these differences in turn have a major impact on the skill requirements and development of managers. Large Japanese firms, for example, with strong internal labor markets and consequently low turnover rates, use systematic job rotation and ongoing training programs to invest in developing a set of general managerial competencies, an undertaking that most U.S. companies would not be willing to support (Dore and Sako 1988).

Stevens (1996) has shown that there is a large intermediate category of "transferable skills," like the understanding of a new computer technology or of a retail distribution system, that are best created primarily under one employer but are potentially useful to a group of companies within a sector. She also showed that market failures for transferable skills can easily arise because firms are unwilling to invest in these skills for fear their employees will be "poached" by competitors. Stevens' third observation is that individuals may be unable to make this investment because of capital constraints, the risks associated with an investment in sector-specific skills that they may lose if they lose their job, and the need to have the cooperation of their firms. Where such market failures exist, one possible solution is for intermediate institutions, such as employer organizations, to bring private sector actors together to form a "club" (in the economist's sense of the term). A *club* is a voluntary association of actors (in this case, firms) who develop a means of restricting access to an otherwise public good, such as a professional association that holds meetings and provides services only to its members. While in free labor markets it is not possible for some firms to restrict the access of others to their employees skills, Olson (1971) has shown how clubs can potentially overcome this barrier to collective action by generating secondary benefits—linked to the provision of transferable skills—that are consumable individually and on a basis of some exclusion, thus giving them some leverage over members (see Crouch, Finegold, and Sako 1999 for a fuller discussion of club theory applied to skill creation). Thus, for example, German chambers of commerce exercise both formal and informal pressure on member firms that are not perceived to be providing their share of places in the apprenticeship system (Streeck 1987; Soskice 1991). Such intermediate institutions are given added legitimacy, and thus hold a greater attraction for potential members, where they are included in corporatist policymaking and given public resources to help attain policy objectives (e.g., Hall 1986).

The alternative solution to market failure problems is for the state to play a role in the development of managers. The state has several theoretical justifications for supporting the development of general managerial skills (particularly in areas where there is a strong public good component to the skills): to ensure individuals have equal access to this important determinant of future life success, to increase the societal stock of knowledge and skills in order to foster economic growth, and to promote a more enlightened citizenry. In reality, however, in both countries the state has taken a major role in the education and training of managers more from historical accident than any strong case of market failure or public good. Publicly funded colleges and universities are the principal providers of higher education in these countries, like the rest of the Organisation for Economic Co-operation and Development (OECD). As the demand for management education from individuals and companies grew following World War II, public colleges and universities responded by developing a variety of courses ranging from undergraduate diplomas and degrees to executive MBAs and short, noncredit modules tailored to specific skill needs.

Given this large existing state role, one of our study's most striking findings was the near universal opposition to any direct state role in management development. While this opposition might have been expected from company managers and individuals in the United States (where government has traditionally been distant from the private sector), more surprising was the equally strong hostility to state intervention in Germany, where over 90 percent of respondents to our interviews did not see a role for the state in the initial or further training of managers. The most frequently cited reasons for why the state is not the most effective provider of management development were 1) public institutions are slow to adapt; 2) companies are in the best position to determine new managerial demands and train for them; 3) managers learn best in "real world" situations; and 4) the returns to management development accrue to the firm and the individual, and therefore it should be financed by them, not the taxpayer. Some respondents went further, arguing that government involvement in management development could actually be counterproductive, because subsidies for public institutions could discourage the development of private providers, while individuals who do not have to pay for management education (as is the case in many publicly funded higher education systems) may not treat it as an investment nor be sufficiently motivated.

Beneath the broad antagonism to direct government involvement in management development, however, was a recognition by interviewees that there are a number of indirect, yet important, ways in which the state contributes to the education and training of managers. Most notable is providing individuals who may eventually become managers with a solid educational foundation on which to build more specific and ever-changing skills. Nearly every respondent indicated that, given limited resources, government's first priority should be ensuring a high-quality basic education for all citizens.

INSTITUTIONAL ARRANGEMENTS FOR MANAGEMENT DEVELOPMENT

Germany

The 90 government-run universities and 125 *Fachhochschulen* (technical colleges) act as the main training ground for future German managers (Table 1). The educational task facing these institutions is simplified by the high-quality general education and demanding entrance exams that all individuals qualifying for higher education must pass so that they can receive a state-funded place that covers tuition and living expenses.

With their extensive and academically oriented coursework, the universities are the traditional pillars of the German higher education system. Courses at the university can theoretically be completed in four to five years, but overcrowding in these institutions has made this difficult in practice. Overcrowding has been caused by a substantial increase in the number of young people qualifying for places over the last two decades (with approximately 30 percent of each cohort now going on to higher education) without a substantial increase in the physical capacity of universities. The result has been an oversubscription of many courses and a lengthening of the average time to graduation to 6.5 years.

Table 1 German Graduates by Academic Discipline, 1991 (in thousands)

Discipline	University	*Fachhochschule*	Total
Language, cultural studies, sport	13.2	1.0	14.2
Law, economics, and social sciences	22.7	26.5	49.2
Mathematics and natural sciences	17.2	2.9	20.1
Engineering	11.8	24.5	36.3
Medicine	11.8	—	11.8
Agricultural	2.5	2.2	4.7
Arts	3.7	1.8	5.5
Total	83.0	58.9	141.9

SOURCE: Bundesministerium für Bildung und Wissenschaft, Grund- und Struktur Daten, 1993–1994.

The active role that the German government plays in regulating higher education was cited by many respondents as the major weakness in the German system of management development. Said one interviewee, "The system [of higher education] puts professors first, students a distant second, and ignores the needs of industry altogether. It needs to be changed to put students in the role of consumers of professional skills and professors in the position of providing a service." Three factors were cited as helping to create a "bureaucratic mentality" and inhibiting innovation among providers of higher education. The first is the way in which curricula are determined. Reorganizing an existing course or introducing a new course at either type of public institution requires several levels of deliberation and consultation, both inside the institution itself and with local educational authorities. The effect is to discourage new ideas. The second factor cited as inhibiting innovation is the professors' status as civil servants with lifetime appointments, which effectively insulates them from having to respond to those who demand marketable skills, e.g., students and firms. A final factor cited as discouraging innovation is disincentives to be active in the area of further training and customized courses in management. Money earned from offering further training courses goes not to the professor, the professor's faculty, or to the university or *Fachhochschule* itself, but rather straight to the state. By removing the financial incentives for involvement in further training, the state has stemmed the flow of ideas between industry and higher education which normally arise from this activity. The result has been to discourage the public institutions of higher education from keeping pace with market developments.

The *Fachhochschulen* were established in the 1960s to accommodate the growing numbers of students going on to higher education and to provide a more relevant course for managers entering industry. As an alternative to the more academic university education, courses at the *Fachhochschulen* are shorter and more vocationally oriented. Coursework is normally completed in three to four years of full-time study, and the average graduation age is a correspondingly younger 24–25. Nearly three-quarters of the students graduate in engineering or business administration, showing the heavily professional orientation of these technical colleges.

The vocational orientation of the *Fachhochschulen* is reinforced through close contact to industry. Fully two-thirds of students at the *Fachhochschulen*, but only one-third of those studying at a university, complete an apprenticeship before going on to higher education.[1] Company-based internships are, moreover, an integral element of the educational experience, with one or more internships of several months required during the period of study. A balance between theory and practice is also institutionalized in instruction. Professors as a rule have several years of hands-on experience in either industry or law, and recruiting visiting professors and guest lecturers from firms is common practice.

Together, graduates of the universities and *Fachhochschulen* hold the majority of management positions at all levels, but with clear variation in the type of position held. While *Fachhochschule* graduates outnumber their university counterparts in the lower levels of management, accounting for 31 percent (compared with 21 percent) of department heads, they are relatively underrepresented in the ranks of top management. More than half of managing director positions are held by university graduates, with only 20 percent of these positions falling to those from the *Fachhochschulen* (Table 2).

In recruiting from the university and *Fachhochschule*, German firms favor graduates with technical as opposed to liberal arts education. Graduates in engineering, economics, and business administration are among the most highly recruited groups. Those students who combine university and traditional apprenticeship are highly sought after by companies for their mix of theoretical and practical training (Table 3). There is a prestige gap between the universities and *Fachhochschulen*, reflected in differences in pay and career prospects for the faculty and graduates of these institutions. This gap may be narrowing, however, as there is a broadly held perception among both policymakers and business people, exemplified by several managers we interviewed, that "university instruction is too long and theoretical and [that] university students are squandering educational resources." This puts the *Fachhochschulen,* with their short, industry-oriented courses, in an increasingly favorable light. The trend in educational policies of several of the large German states was to increase resources for the *Fachhochschulen*, with the goal of changing the student ratio from 70:30 in favor of the universities to 50:50 by the year 2000.

Table 2 Educational Qualifications of German Managers, 1990 (%)

	Managing directors	First level (division head)	Second level (department head)
University	52[a]	33	21
Polytechnic (economic studies)	7	8	8
Polytechnic (technical studies)	13	18	23
Abitur (upper secondary certificate)	9	8	5
Middle exam	10	20	21
Other	9	13	22

SOURCE: Kienbaum und Partner, compensation survey, 1990.
[a] Sixteen percent of managing directors have a doctorate in addition to their university degree.

Table 3 Academic Disciplines of Employed University and Polytechnic Graduates (%)

	1983	1993[a]	Managing directors
Engineering	43	43	35
Economics/business administration	35	38	44
Natural sciences	11	12	10
Other	11	7	11

SOURCE: Institut der deutschen WirtschaftFirm Questionnaire 1982; Kienbaum Compensation Survey 1993.
[a] Projections to 1993.

The importance of educational attainment for a management career varies considerably according to firm size and among economic sectors. Among the largest and most internationally active German companies, there is great respect for academic attainment. Over half of the managing directors of the largest 100 German firms possess a doctorate in engineering, science, or law. Recruits from universities are also more likely than *Fachhochschule* graduates to find their way into large companies' "high-potential" management training programs.

Fachhochschule graduates are, on the other hand, coveted by firms in the German *Mittelstand*, the small- and medium-sized manufacturing enterprises that have accounted for much of the nation's export success. Typically operating on a tight budget, these firms do not have the time nor the internal resources to bring the "high-potential" university graduates up to speed. The *Fachhochschule*-trained engineers or economists are attractive to small- or medium-sized enterprises (SMEs) because their more practical education allows them to dive right into work.

An equally pronounced split in patterns of management, recruiting, and promotion is found between firms in the manufacturing and service sectors and those in the services. Whereas in the traditional strongholds of German industry (e.g., chemicals, auto) reaching top management is very difficult without a university degree (and in some cases a doctorate) in services, only a few sectors, such as large consulting firms, recruit managers and professionals exclusively from the ranks of university graduates. Finding individuals in most service firms with the *Fachwirt* or *Fachkaufleute* (advanced and vocational certificates, respectively) as their highest level of educational attainment in the ranks of top management is quite normal. The large banks are the service sector firms most thoroughly infiltrated by university graduates and yet only 25 percent of the managerial workforce and 50 percent of top managers are graduates, although they are now recruiting more university graduates as the number of young people participating in higher education has increased. In the hotel and retail sectors, the number of graduates in the ranks of management is considerably smaller (e.g., approximately 10 and 5 percent, respectively).

The United States

In contrast to the situation in Germany, the U.S. federal government has been a relatively minor player in education generally and management development in particular, with the primary responsibility resting with state and local governments and private actors (individuals and firms). The federal government accounts for under 8 percent of total spending on compulsory education, and, unlike most other advanced industrial countries, has no national standards for education.[2] Federal funding for higher education has been more substantial and helped the United States construct the world's first mass higher education system. A combination of means-tested federal grants and loans to individuals, private scholarships, and funding for large public universities has helped make some form of higher education an affordable option for the majority of Americans. But in contrast to Germany, this funding comes with relatively minimal regulation of institutions or qualifications, allowing universities virtually complete freedom to design courses and compete for students in the higher education marketplace.

The result of this decentralized system has been that the quantity of education in the United States is impressive, even if the quality of some educational programs (notably the high school diploma) is highly variable compared with that of other nations (Handy 1987). International comparisons of educational attainment of both high school students and adults in the workplace find that mean U.S. scores rank in the middle of the pack, but the United States has the widest dispersion of any of the advanced industrial countries, with some of the best and worst performing individuals (Colvin and Shorgren 1997; OECD 1996). More than 80 percent of the adult population aged 25–64 has a high school diploma or equivalent certificate, and nearly two-thirds of young adults aged 20–24 in the United States enroll in a community college, college, or university (International Institute for Management Development 1993). The high levels of education of the U.S. population compared with those of other industrialized countries are presented in Table 4.

Eighty-five percent of all U.S. employees have at least a high school diploma, and among the ranks of persons who classify themselves as managers and professionals, 96 percent have high school diplomas and 47 percent have at least undergraduate degrees (data from U.S. Current Population Survey 1990). Table 5 presents the percentages of managers, professionals, and general employees who have achieved the highest levels of education across all industries. There is wide variation among business sectors. For example, in financial services, 52 percent of managers have college degrees, whereas in the construction sector, only 26 percent of managers have degrees. Among U.S. college students, business administration remains the most popular subject concentration; nearly one quarter of all students major in business, an option which grew in popularity throughout the 1980s

Table 4 Population Percentage Completing Different Levels of Education (%)

	United States	OECD average
Early childhood (K–8)	17	45
Upper secondary (9–12; high school)	47	36
Higher education (university and other)	36	19
Total	100	100

SOURCE: OECD 1993.

Table 5 Percentage of All U.S. Workers and Managers Completing Various Levels of Education (%)

	High school dropout	High school graduate	Some college	College graduate	Post-graduate	All levels
Managerial/professional	4	26	23	30	17	100
All others	17	47	22	10	4	100
Total workforce	15	44	22	13	6	100

SOURCE: Current Population Survey 1991.
[a] Managers and professionals represent 17 percent of the total working population.

(National Center for Education Statistics 1995). U.S. young people, who have to self-finance a larger portion of their higher education than do their European counterparts, place an emphasis on acquiring practical, marketable skills while in college. As one career placement officer explained, "The kids now are already thinking about finding jobs when they graduate. If it isn't going to help them get and keep a good job, they don't want to bother, and they switch or leave."

Outside of formal education, the state has not historically supported professional development within U.S. firms, other than allowing companies to deduct training costs from operating expenses before taxes. The Clinton administration launched a network of Manufacturing Technology and Extension Centers, similar to the Rationalization Committee of German Industry (RKW) though more limited in scope, which help small firms improve their product and process technology

(Finegold et al. 1994). Much of the service these centers provide is essentially management development for SMEs, enabling them to redesign their organizations and upskill their workforces.

State governments have played a more direct role in management development and worker training. The level and type of government support varies widely across the 50 states (Batt and Osterman 1993). The growth in state-subsidized customized training is part of a general trend toward integration of education and training and economic development at the state level. North and South Carolina, for example, have used training packages provided by their technical colleges to become leaders in attracting new businesses. Iowa and Oklahoma have programs that allow eligible firms to fund their training expenses through the issuance of bonds that are underwritten by the state. The funds can be used to train new workers or retrain existing workers, with community colleges and private consultants usually providing the training. If, after the training, the firm shows an increase in profits, some or all of the interest and principal payments are forgiven by the state. The reasoning is that effective training should have a positive effect on the bottom-line financial results of the company, and if this happens, the firm is contributing more in state taxes, which thus allows the training to effectively pay for itself.

Likewise, Arizona recently enacted state support for professional development as an incentive for companies to create new jobs. A fund of $3 million is set aside each year which corporations can apply for if they are expanding their Arizona operation or relocating to the state. In either case, they must be adding new jobs. Twenty percent of the pool has been set aside each year to assist small companies (less than 100 total employees). A common aspect to all the programs described is that although the government provides funding and clear guidelines for eligibility and repayment, it does not directly provide the retraining. Firms are free to contract with education providers, both public and private, to design and build the courses they deem the most worthwhile. These state and federal initiatives, while growing, are still relatively minor in the context of overall U.S. management development.

German Intermediate Institutions

Though university and *Fachhochschule* graduates account for the majority of German managers, there is a sizable minority who have not been through higher education. A look back at Table 2 shows nongraduates to be well represented at all levels of management, accounting for half of the department heads, over 40 percent of the division heads, and some 30 percent of the managing directors. For the nongraduates, entry into management is normally contingent upon achieving a second level of vocational qualification. These qualifications build on the completion of an apprenticeship and a minimum of 3–5 years of work experience, and, like apprenticeships, this route into management is made possible by strong employer organizations (such as the 83 chambers of commerce and industry which all German employers are required to join). The chambers oversee these courses and administer the final certifying exam, ensuring the relevance of course content to employer needs and a consistent quality standard across the country.

Referred to as *Aufstiegsweiterbildung* (literally, promotion-oriented further training), this second level of vocational qualification is represented by the *Meister* (master craftsman or supervisor) certificate in industry and the *Fachwirt* or *Fachkaufleute* certificates in services. Every year thousands of individuals complete *Meister*, *Fachwirt*, and *Fachkaufleute* courses and the associated exams in a broad range of disciplines across all industrial and commercial sectors (see Table 4). For each type of further training, classroom instruction is offered in the evenings or on weekends and is meant to accompany continued work, with the goal of achieving a tight integration of theory and practice. The courses involve between 500–900 hours of classroom-based instruction, spread out over a two- to three-year period, and costs range from DM 2500–6000 ($1,500–3,500), which in some cases are paid by the employing firm.

Despite these similarities, each course plays a different role in Germany's system of management education. Of the three, it is *Fachwirt* courses that have the strongest claim to being management education. While the *Fachkaufleute* certificate is designed to deepen the skills and knowledge of lower- and middle-level managers in the administrative function, the *Fachwirt* is often considered a prerequisite for those without a university degree to move into management, especially in larger service firms. After successfully completing the *Fachwirt* exam, individuals typically take over responsibility for a small business unit within a larger commercial firm, e.g., a bank's branch office or the purchasing group within a department store. Later, opportunities for movement into higher levels of management for *Fachwirt* graduates, including top management, are also abundant.

The analog to the *Fachwirt* in industry, the *Meister* courses, are designed to prepare the skilled manufacturing worker to take over a leadership position in production. Just over half of instruction is devoted to deepening technical knowledge and understanding of manufacturing processes. Technical training is complemented with courses in business administration, along with instruction in pedagogical and organizational issues. *Meister* certificate holders not only supervise other employees and organize production but also play a critical role in continuous skill formation on the shop floor. It is these individuals who oversee the training of apprentices.

With the move toward flatter, more team-based organizations, the traditional role of the supervisor—to maintain control over production—declines in importance (Mason 1996), but this has not decreased German firms' need for individuals with *Meister* qualifications (Finegold and Wagner 1997). They continue to encourage skilled workers to pursue the *Meister* qualification as the demand increases for persons doing more long-range technical and organizational planning activities: design and monitoring of quality control systems (e.g., obtaining and requalifying for ISO 9001); leading continuous improvement efforts; acting as a representative of manufacturing on integrated product teams (IPTs); serving as programmers; or working as a technical expert within the team. To better equip *Meister* holders for the new work environment, the standards and curriculum for their courses have been reformed with further emphasis on communication, cooperation, planning, technical, and coaching skills (Scholz 1996).

For those who have successfully completed a *Meister* course, opportunities for upward mobility are considerably more limited than for their counterparts in services. Among large manufacturers, *Meister* holders have traditionally been unable to rise above the level of supervisor. However, while in the relatively flat employment hierarchy of the small- or medium-sized firm, the *Meister* is on the same level of the employment hierarchy as the managers of other functional departments (sales, personnel, or quality control), many of whom are graduates of a university or *Fachhochschule*. As larger firms downsize, the *Meister* holders who remain are often the only management layer between the plant manager and the shopfloor.

In addition to the role that chambers of commerce play in supporting further training, there is another quasi-public organization active in the field of management development—the Rationalization Committee of German Industry (RKW)—from which German SMEs also derive considerable benefits. Since its founding in 1923, the RKW has focused on assisting economic rationalization and structural adjustment in the German economy, with particular attention to the needs of small- and medium-sized manufacturing firms. Through its central office in Frankfurt and regional offices in each of the federal states, the RKW offers a range of services oriented toward supporting innovative management in the German *Mittelstand*. One service is delivering ongoing training courses in management education. A second is onsite consulting in organization flexibility, implementing new technology, and controlling budgets. In 1992, the RKW logged some 43,500 days of consulting work in just over 6,000 different firms (RKW 1992). A final service offered by the RKW is the publication of books and expert reports on themes related to innovation management. Drawing on the expertise of business practitioners, university professors, and other management experts, the RKW produces 25–30 publications each year covering innovations in technology, organization, and personnel development.

The benefits of the chambers' and the RKW's activities to the SMEs are twofold. The most obvious is the increased availability of management training and consulting. Because of public subsidies to both types of organizations, these services can be obtained by the SME at a price as much as one-third below market value. Less obvious, but perhaps more important, is the role both organizations play in diffusing innovative management techniques (Wever 1995). For the RKW, extensive involvement with small business enterprises permits a steady accumulation of knowledge about evolving management practices, knowledge which in turn can be diffused through consulting and publishing activities. The chambers' involvement in *Aufstiegsweiterbildung* leads to extensive interaction with both large and small firms, contact which allows for the accumulation of expertise that again can be diffused.

Employers' organizations also play a role in supporting the management development efforts of SMEs through networks of private training providers. These providers are of two sorts. One called the Training Center of German Industry resembles the RKW in organizational form. It operates through regional administrative bodies in each of the federal states. The second type of private provider with strong links to employers' organizations is professional associations. These are organized on an industry basis and include the Association for Professional Education in Banking, the Institute for Professional Education in Retail Trade, and the Training Guild for Metalworkers.

U.S. Intermediate Institutions

The United States has numerous employer and professional organizations, but in comparison with Germany's, these intermediate institutions are relatively weak. They lack the compulsory membership or regulatory supports that allow their German counterparts to act as strategic players in the corporatist policy formulation, which helps overcome public goods problems (see Crouch, Finegold, and Sako 1999); instead, they typically play two roles: providing services, such as management development in competition with other providers in the marketplace, and lobbying for their members in policy debates.

The American Management Association (AMA) provides an example of a large U.S. labor market intermediary. It is the largest and one of the oldest private providers of management seminars in the world. Founded in 1923, the AMA has over 70,000 members, including many in Europe, most of whom are business managers. The AMA offers two types of short seminars, three- to five-day courses for mid-level managers and one- to two-day courses for office administrators and supervisors. The AMA contracts with independent consultants to teach the courses. The breadth of subjects offered in AMA seminars covers every area of management, both general and industry-specific, as well as technical and "soft" subjects. Among the most popular current offerings are courses on implementing information technology, ISO 9000 quality standards, workforce diversity, power speaking, inventory management, and increasing customer satisfaction.

Although the AMA fulfills a role similar to that of the RKW, it is a nonprofit educational institution that funds itself strictly through course fees and sales of journals and books it publishes. The president of the AMA states the reasons for this: "We not only don't seek government assistance, we don't accept it when offered. If we can't run our own business successfully, how can we expect to help our members and clients run theirs?" Reflecting this private-sector orientation, there appears to be a strong preference in AMA courses for business practitioners rather than academics to serve as faculty.

THE GERMAN MARKET FOR MANAGEMENT DEVELOPMENT

The strong role of the state and employer organizations in Germany has had many beneficial effects, most notably ensuring that individuals and firms, regardless of their financial resources, have access to management development. As noted, however, the entrenched higher education bureaucracy lacks market-like mechanisms that can stimulate innovation and responsiveness to customer demands in the public sector. A good example of the negative impact that the state has had on the potential market for management development is the Master of Business Administration (MBA). Despite significant demand, an MBA was still not an officially recognized educational degree in the Federal Republic at the end of the 1980s, and thus no German educational institution offered the degree. In the 1990s, however, public and private universities found ways around this lack of recognition, awarding MBAs in conjunction with a sister school abroad or by renaming MBA-style courses (i.e., those with case studies, team projects, and company internships) with such titles as Master in International Business. There are now close to 15 German institutions offering one- to two-year MBA-style programs, and between 600–800 German students take the MBA degree each year, with approximately half of those degrees earned abroad (Haller 1993). The international orientation of the degree is a key to explaining the rapid growth in interest in the MBA (Schneider 1993). International management topics and opportunities to study at sister schools abroad form core elements of most

German MBA programs and set the MBA apart from the normal business administration courses found at the universities and *Fachhochschulen*.

A few select, private universities are most highly regarded for their instruction in this area. The Koblenz School of Corporate Management, the European School of Management in Berlin, and the European Business School in Oestrich-Winkel are similar to their public counterparts in offering a number of different final degrees in the area of business administration. Their business administration courses are developed in the context of international business, with topics like international marketing, finance, and personnel management making up the core elements of instruction. Coursework on international business themes is also complemented with periods spent studying and completing company-based internships abroad.

There are a few other private management training providers in Germany, but those with close ties to employers' associations are certainly the most important. One factor that has stifled the creation of a more active market for management development is the lack of demand from firms. Small firms, as noted above, rely heavily on quasi-public institutions and the chambers for assistance, while large firms typically outsource far less management development than their U.S. counterparts; large German companies keep 90 percent of ongoing training internal, using external providers for specialty classes, particularly in the area of information technology. In contrast, large U.S. companies typically spend more than 60 percent of their development expenditure on outside experts (Weiss 1994; Bassi and Cheney 1996).

THE U.S. MARKET FOR MANAGEMENT DEVELOPMENT

Unlike Germany, the United States has a thriving market for further management development, epitomized by its business schools that attract students from all over the world to obtain the highly prized MBA (Finegold and Brewer 1996). In U.S. business, demonstrated ability counts for more than academic credentials, but increasingly, U.S. managers believe the two are connected. Thus, almost all U.S. managers in large organizations now start their careers with a degree (usually business or technical) that they later augment with further management study and/or an MBA. Of the six sectors studied, only hotel managers did not think a university degree was an important entry characteristic or a prerequisite for promotion beyond a certain level. The other exception to the rule of degreed managers is at start-up firms, where entrepreneurs often see little or no payoff from formal higher education.

While only 10–12 percent of all managers in business have MBAs, 35 percent of chief executives of America's largest 500 companies possess them. The MBA originated in the United States in the late nineteenth century (Porter and McKibbon 1985). Until the Wharton School of Business was founded at the University of Pennsylvania in 1881, business education in the United States had been the province of technical schools and commercial colleges. The MBA gained in prestige in the early twentieth century as world-renowned institutions such as Harvard and Stanford added graduate business schools. By the mid twentieth century, the classic MBA—with its full-time, two-year curriculum of management, accounting, finance, and operations, and an emphasis on quantitative analysis—was well established. The average student worked 2–3 years before seeking an MBA, and the goal of the MBA was to produce a new breed of general manager, educated to a graduate level in all aspects of running a business. Still, MBAs were relatively rare, with only 4,500 awarded in 1956 and just nine schools accounting for more than half of all the degrees awarded. The growth in the popularity of MBAs since then has been explosive, particularly throughout the 1970s and 1980s. In 1991, over 78,000 MBAs were awarded by over 700 American business schools.

The recession of the early 1990s slowed the growth in MBAs for the first time, with the number of persons taking the Graduate Management Admissions Test (GMAT), which is the standard entrance exam for MBA applicants, declining from 1990–1993. Much of the decline was cyclical, reflecting the substantial downsizing of many large U.S. corporations, including the reduction in layers of management (Lawler, Mohrman, and Ledford 1995), but complaints from companies about the usefulness of MBAs were also increasing. Until fairly recently, "classic" American business education emphasized analytics and finance and was U.S.-centric in its focus. This traditional education has been criticized as being shortsighted and inadequate to meet the

increased pressures on businesses today. A new set of business competencies is augmenting (but not replacing) the old: foreign language
skills, familiarity with other cultures, Internet literacy, and firm-based
team projects, for example. These important additions to business
school curricula are a reaction to critics who charged that business
schools were not adapting quickly enough to changes in the duties and
career structures of managers (Haynes 1991).

A sign of the market responsiveness of U.S. business schools was
that as soon as demand for their educational products began to slacken,
institutions adopted major reforms. Most of the top-tier MBA programs have reengineered themselves in the last 5–10 years. While
many of these reforms are still in their early phases, the more promi-
nent changes include a greater emphasis on teamwork and firm-based
learning, greater international experience, and use of new technologies.
The contrast between the elements of the traditional MBA model and
the new model, which the top-tier business schools are adopting, is
shown in Table 6 (see Finegold et al. 1994 for fuller discussion). The
reforms, along with the turnaround of the U.S. economy, have helped
produce a resurgence in demand for MBAs, with applications and starting salaries at record levels (Lord 1997).

Another factor driving changes in MBA programs has been the
shifting demographics of the customer base. The average starting age

Table 6 Changes under Way in U.S. MBA Programs

Traditional model	New model
Few courses	Diversify provision
Classroom-based	Apprenticeship
Theoretical	Real-world cases
Finance, quantitative focus	Analytic and soft ("people") skills
Functional separation	Cross-functional
Faculty focus on research	Balance research & teaching emphasis
U.S.-centric	International
Individualistic/competitive	Group/cooperative
Male-dominated student body	Diverse (women, minorities) student body
Early in career	Lifelong learning
Traditional lectures	Use of new technologies

for full-time MBA students was 24–25 ten years ago; now it is 27. Business school officials and firms we interviewed agreed that more work experience (and greater maturity) make the MBA a more valuable academic experience. Most business schools have developed new course options—part-time MBAs, FMBA (fully employed MBA), and EMBA (executive MBA)—to cater to students who are already in the workplace. These programs offer similar coursework to the full-time programs but are structured to accommodate students' work schedules. Students meet nights and weekends for their classes while working during the week. Unlike full-time MBAs, firms, rather than the individuals themselves, often pay the tuition and related costs.

Another sign of the ways in which business schools and other U.S. providers of management development have responded to changes in demand is the dramatic growth in customized training. This firm-specific training uses the business problems faced by the company as course material and incorporates the firm's business requirements and strategy, rather than focusing on the general development of the individual. The growth in customized training occurred when companies began to question the economic returns to the company from costly executive education or other general-audience short courses. While it "may pay off for the individual participant, there is little evidence of how such education has increased the value of the business corporations," according to Finegold et al. (1994). "Companies are using executive education," they continue, "to meet specific strategic goals or transform corporate culture; organizational transformation is replacing a focus on personal development."

In custom courses, the education provider—usually business school executive education departments, community college professional development centers, or private providers—tailors coursework to the business needs of individual companies and teaches only selected managers and professionals from that company, often onsite. The courses may be only a few days or part of an ongoing partnership between the provider and the firm. The educator may access proprietary information that requires confidentiality agreements or similar guarantees. In the past, leading business schools have resisted customizing courses, but that now appears to be changing. At many schools, customized courses have increased from 10 to 40 percent of the executive education department's revenues over the past three years and demand is still growing.

Smaller companies and companies seeking to retrain large segments of their workforce are more likely to seek their customized training from more affordable and accessible community colleges, which provide a state-subsidized service somewhat similar to the RKW in Germany. One of the community colleges in our sample had a professional development center that had trained individuals in hundreds of SMEs. Most of the training is customized total quality management (TQM) and statistical process control (SPC) courses, which the college provided on the firm's premises after performing an analysis of the company's specific business needs. The companies often use the training to initiate an effort to transform the business processes and culture of their organizations. Participants in the initial training cohort are purposely selected to represent a cross-section of all the major business functions and levels within the organization; for example, trainees may include the head of accounting, a mid-level operations professional, and someone from marketing. When the class is over, the skills acquired can be utilized on the job and shared with other co-workers, who may become part of a later training cohort.

Private providers, such as the AMA and Globecon, have also added or increased the customized component of their training. At the AMA, the newest division, AMA On-Site, is the fastest growing. AMA On-Site provides week-long courses at the customer's own facility that are tailored versions of AMA's general seminars. Globecon has carved a successful niche by combining consulting and education services to "solve a bank's overall business problems, rather than just their training needs," according to its president. While this plethora of U.S. providers creates a wide array of options for individuals and firms who want to purchase management development in the marketplace, it can also create problems. The lack of standards and rapid rate of change led many of the managers we interviewed to complain about the difficulty of determining the quality and relevance of the many courses that are offered.

GERMAN FIRMS

Compared with the system of initial management education, firm-based management development in Germany can only be described as weak. German firms rely on hiring already qualified individuals from universities and *Aufstiegsweiterbildung* courses and then do relatively little to train them further. As one management recruiter said, "We expect [applicants] to bring their certificates with them . . . [and] possession of these certificates attained through a long course of training will allow them to get on with the job."

What this means for the great majority of German managers is that further development efforts are minimal. One survey of over 800 large- and medium-sized firms estimated that German managers spend three to five days per year on further training in courses mainly devoted to "soft" management themes like motivation and communication (Gaugler and Witz 1993). The survey of European Union (EU) member states also found that German enterprises were the least likely in the EU to use systematic job rotation or periods spent abroad as tools of management development. A mere 7 percent of German firms used employment abroad as part of their personnel development, putting German industry last in the EU and considerably below the EU average of 17 percent. Only 12 percent of German firm respondents had job rotation programs, again a figure well below the EU average of 25 percent.

Alongside the lack of investment in ongoing management development are structural features of German firms that may hinder their transition to more team-oriented forms of work and the accompanying development of new managerial capabilities (Wever 1995; Herrigel 1996). There are two reasons for expecting difficulties. The first is the residual hierarchy of German industry. This manifests itself in a preoccupation with certifying and ranking skill levels, e.g., the university over the *Fachhochschule,* and the *Meister* certificate over the skilled worker. It also appears in the emphasis German managers at all levels place on technical expertise as the basis for their authority. These ways of ranking skill levels make the transition to fluid organizational structures difficult to implement. A second barrier to creating teams is the minimal use of job rotation by German firms for the purposes of personnel development. Because most managers, unlike apprentices, do not have opportunities to cultivate their skills in different functional areas, they may be less adequately prepared to organize and lead teams of functional experts.

The comparative neglect of management development by German industry is confirmed by other studies (Wever 1995). One survey of German and British middle managers showed a strong pattern of functional management in German firms. Of the 30 German managers surveyed, all but one had stayed in the same functional area during the entire period with his present employer. Twenty of these managers had been in the same position for more than 5 years, and 12 of them more than 10 years. Another comparison of the career patterns of German and Japanese managers suggested that 10 times as many Japanese managers had made rotations through Germany as German managers through Japan.[3]

Opportunities for sustained investment in management development are, in fact, open to only a small and elite group of the managerial workforce in large German firms. These programs identify "high-potential" management candidates and intensively cultivate the next generation of top managers. As one executive stated, "It is these individuals who will make the organization prosper, and so cultivating their leadership and business skills is the highest priority." High-potential programs typically consist of two elements. The first is job rotation through different functional departments, product divisions, and international operations. Switching employment positions relatively frequently (e.g., two- to five-year rotations) allows the "top manager in training" not only to develop a sense for the company's overall business but also to demonstrate a high level of initiative and commitment to the firm. Among the managers we interviewed, periods spent working abroad were considered particularly critical to developing the skills and flexibility needed for leadership positions.

Further training complements job rotation for this elite group. "The purpose of further training," said one developer, "is to take the normal manager and turn him into an entrepreneur and business leader." It is typically only the high-potential candidates who attend training seminars in subjects like entrepreneurship and strategic management, as well as international marketing and personnel management, at such notable providers as the German *Universitätsseminar der*

Wirtschaft (USW). Europe's top-rated business school, the European Institute of Business Administration (INSEAD) at Fontainebleau, and the Harvard Business School also play a role in further training top managers. For some firms, the external seminars are considered very important; they are expected to stimulate creativity by giving top managers distance from the organization and putting them in contact with other business leaders. Most organizations, however, consider external seminars too highly priced to be cost-effective and, as noted earlier, German companies typically outsource far less management development than their U.S. counterparts.

In size and degree of formalization, the high-potential programs vary somewhat from industry to industry. We found that the largest number of managers designated as "high potential" worked in large banks and high-technology manufacturing. They represented close to 10 percent of all managers. These firms also had a relatively high degree of structure in their further training, with clearly laid-out training programs accompanying upward mobility. Among hotels and lower-tech manufacturers (e.g., food processing), the development programs were less formal and smaller, including only 1–3 percent of the management workforce.

U.S. FIRMS

In-company training, both formal and especially informal, is the most common mode of management development in the United States. It is also considered most practical because new competencies can be developed as necessary. U.S. employers spend over $40 billion each year on additional training, with a high percentage spent on management training in particular (Fuchsberg 1993). Lillard and Tan (1986) showed that the likelihood of getting formal on-the-job training and the amount of that training rise with the level of schooling.

Formal training is most common at the onset of employment in a large firm. At this time, a high-potential new recruit is likely to enter a management development program that includes some classwork and systematic job rotations. After formal initiation, which lasts anywhere from six months to two years, in-company training becomes less programmatic and more individualized. Large companies increasingly include in their annual personnel performance assessments a section where the individual and his or her supervisors can decide what skills the employee needs to develop and how best to develop them. The individual development plan resulting from this process may include specific new responsibilities, course attendance, and rotations in different departments or divisions. Also, the provision of certain seminars or courses is often standard when a manager reaches certain levels or is assigned to certain departments.

A growing number of large U.S. firms have formalized in-company training and extended it to all the employees of the firm and its suppliers by establishing corporate universities. Firms such as Motorola, General Electric, and Xerox have developed autonomous business units whose primary function is to meet their company's ambitious continuous education requirements. These corporate universities combine the use of education to meet specific strategic goals or achieve organizational transformation with a strong, ongoing commitment to professional development. Because of the level of resources required to set up these universities, they tend to be limited to very large companies.

Motorola University (MU), arguably the most well-known company university, is more of a planner and contractor than a training provider. The mission of MU is to provide the means by which Motorola's 120,000 employees, worldwide, can continuously upgrade their skills. To accomplish this mission, MU has units at the main Motorola facilities, including in China, sometimes forming partnerships with local colleges to deliver courses. For example, classes at MU's western division are administered by Mesa Community College, which screens and hires course instructors, provides classrooms and support services, and administers course registration. By charter, MU only develops its own courses if the subject is not obtainable through a local college or private provider or if it requires discussion of proprietary information.

Motorola finds that the benefits provided by MU far outweigh its costs, despite spending over $100 million annually on training in 1992. First, MU courses provide the opportunity continually to restate strategic objectives such as quality improvement, cycle time reduction, and technology leadership, aimed at achieving total customer satisfaction. Second, MU can respond to changing objectives much more quickly and cohesively than outside educational providers. Arnie Sabel, manager of MU West, estimates that about 70 percent of the courses changed in the program's first eight years. The slower pace at which many universities worldwide have responded to the changing business environment is thus notably absent in corporate universities such as MU.

However, for Americans who are not working in the relatively small group of large companies that are leading providers of management development, the United States does not have a highly structured system of training for entry-level managers equivalent to the German *Aufstiegsweiterbildung*. The quantity and quality of management development for this group is thus far more variable, with some individuals receiving no formal management development, while others undertake extensive, ongoing training. The most common approach to further training for supervisors is informal on-the-job training supplemented by short, externally provided courses that individuals or firms purchase in the training marketplace when they have a perceived skill need (Mason and Finegold 1997; Mason 1996). Each course usually focuses on a particular issue or skill set. Some may be industry-specific, such as short courses for bankers on subjects such as credit analysis and securities-backed financing. Other courses, such as those in presentation skills and quality assurance, may be applicable across industries.

Courses last anywhere from a day to two weeks, with costs ranging from $100 for a day-long community college seminar to $15,000 for an executive seminar offered through a business school. To help individuals who take these courses in their own time, a large number of U.S. employers, including many small firms, now offer some form of tuition reimbursement to their employees (Finegold and Mason 1996). In the public transportation industry, for example, 61 percent of all agencies offer tuition reimbursement to supervisors and 55 percent offer it to mechanics (Finegold et al. 1996).

CONCLUSIONS AND POLICY IMPLICATIONS

Our comparison of management development in the United States and Germany reveals a number of conclusions about the role of national institutional structures in the skill-creation process. First, it confirms the findings of earlier international comparisons focused on lower-level skills by showing the important role that different institutional arrangements play in determining the level, type, and effectiveness of skill investment in different countries. Americans and Germans generally learn the skills they need to manage in quite distinct ways, and the choices they and their firms make about what skills to develop and how to develop them are shaped by the incentives, information, and developmental routes created by the national institutional environment.

Second, our research suggests that for a complex set of competencies like those required by modern-day managers, it is wrong to think of a country as having a single or dominant institutional model of skill development, such as the dual system for apprentices or state-based compulsory education. Rather, managers in both countries acquire their skills through a combination of four different institutional arrangements: the state, the market, internal firm hierarchies, and employer or professional organizations. Third, the particular mix of institutional arrangements for management development found in each country is not the result of a market generating the theoretically optimum skill outcome. Neither is it a carefully crafted solution by public policymakers to the challenges facing managers entering the twenty-first century. Instead, the current institutional arrangements demonstrate the strong influence of history or the path-dependent nature of institutional development. Most notably, the large role that the state plays in initial management development, particularly in Germany, is a by-product of the evolution of a government-dominated higher education system.

Finally, it is the fit between the historical mix of institutional arrangements in each country and the types of skills required in the workplace that appears to explain the relative effectiveness of the United States and German systems. Several features of managerial competencies suggest that a combination of individuals investing in their own skills in the marketplace and internal firm development provides the most efficient means of managerial development. The characteristics that appear to favor market-based institutional arrangements over state-led managerial skills development include increasingly dynamic global competition, technological change, and the high rate of private return to market-based skill investment. The returns are also greater if skills development and the timing of the training are closely linked to the managerial requirements of the organization in which the skills will be used. There are, however, a number of reasons why the market alone will fail to provide a sufficient level of investment in transferable managerial skills: imperfect information, capital constraints on individuals or small firms, a lack of internal firm capacity for effective management development, and the free-rider problem. To remedy such deficiencies, it is useful to have strong employer or professional organizations capable of collective action. These organizations can act as an effective conduit for state support for management development, overcoming market failures while at the same ensuring the relevance of the skills created to their members. The respective strengths and weaknesses of the German and U.S. institutional arrangements for management development are summarized below.

Germany

The hallmark of the German management model is a commitment to professional preparation. Through a combination of theoretical and practical training provided by the state and strong intermediate institutions, the vast majority of managers can develop a very deep and rich understanding of their intended area of professional expertise. For students at the *Fachhochschulen*, as well as those at private universities, the combination of theory and practice is a standard part of the curriculum. For university graduates, completion of an apprenticeship and/or a management training program is increasingly used to complement their stricter theoretical training with hands-on experience. The *Meister*, *Fachwirt*, and *Fachkaufleute* courses ensure, moreover, that it is not just top managers, but also those at lower and middle levels of corporations who are comprehensively prepared for their jobs. The courses round out practical work experience with a more theoretical treatment of subjects related to supervision and management.

The emphasis on thorough initial training, a historical strength of the German system, may now be becoming a weakness. It has encouraged German firms to rely heavily on external mechanisms for management skill development and to concentrate their own development efforts on a select group of high-potential recruits. In the process, the functional or "single-career" management model became the accepted paradigm. Rapid economic and technological change mean, however, that the single-career model has become outdated as firms place greater emphasis on the need for functional breadth and continuous learning. In the emerging world economy, therefore, the high-quality initial management training received by most German managers will be a strength only if this acquired skill set can be continually expanded and upgraded.

The German case also suggests the advantages of public support for private initiative and the dangers of public regulation in the area of management development. Employer-dominated institutions such as the chambers of commerce and the RKW enable firms to act cooperatively to drive change using public policy in a supporting role. Further training courses are developed informally in conjunction with private industry. Consulting and other advising activities are likewise oriented toward meeting market demand. Public policy relies on employer organizations and other intermediate institutions to encourage and hasten the diffusion of innovation. Government support gives these organizations a degree of independence from the vagaries of the market, allowing them to continue their activities through recessions. By lowering the costs of training and consulting activities, government subsidies also allow these nonprofit organizations to reach a larger number of firms, including those that would not otherwise invest in management development.

In contrast to its positive role in supporting firm-based management development, the state bureaucracy appears to have hindered innovation in initial and graduate management education. Among the regulations that stifle competition are a cumbersome government approval process that limits the ability of institutions to respond to changing demands by developing new courses; a centralized admissions process that prevents universities from competing for the most able students; and civil service rules governing faculty salaries that limit the incentives for professors to work closely with industry. The large public sector has also crowded out, or at least significantly reduced, the development of a thriving private sector in management development. Not surprisingly, most innovations have come from outside the public educational system in the form of private university education and MBA programs. Management developers and university professors alike agreed that the present system of management education could be improved by higher levels of competition between providers.

The United States

The U.S. case illustrates both the strengths and weaknesses of a more market-driven approach to management development. Individuals, firms, and educators are the primary actors in this system; the government does not play a significant role. Individuals and firms are the initiators of, payers for, and beneficiaries of management education; they are also the source of demand in the system. Colleges and private training institutions supply management education in response to the changing business environment. Firms are becoming increasingly dominant players in the professional development marketplace. Because they are the largest source of funding for postemployment training, firms exercise great power in determining course offerings. In recent years, businesses have been demanding more customized training (or otherwise requiring that training be more firm-specific) in order to receive a greater return on their professional development investment.

The government does play a minor role in the management education marketplace, especially where public investment in training is viewed as a means of retaining or attracting business. The federal role is largely confined to student loans for low-income groups. States subsidize education and training while allowing firms and individuals to make the actual decisions about which schools to choose, how courses should be offered, and who should receive training. Where states have launched training programs, they have attempted to increase the return on this investment by tying the funding to demonstrated results. This approach fosters competition among trainers, flexibility of provision, and less bureaucracy while avoiding the crowding out of private trainers and slow rates of response to changing demands. But, in the absence of regulation and national skill standards, it is often difficult for individuals or firms to ascertain the quality or impact of the many courses offered in the marketplace. Likewise, reliance on the market can exclude those actors—whether economically disadvantaged students or some small firms—that do not have the resources to invest in management development.

Notes

1. Most *Fachhochschule* students take an apprenticeship instead of staying on in school to complete the *Abitur*, the academic upper secondary qualification, although a growing percentage now do both.
2. Under the Clinton administration, however, national standards for education in the United States are being seriously debated for the first time.
3. In a presentation to the *Deutsch-Japanischer Wirtschaftskreis* in Dusseldorf in May 1995, a Japanese manager put the comparative figures at 40,000 and 4,000. An official of the *Wirtschaftskreis* said that "exact figures cannot be verified, but that there were certainly many more Japanese managers coming to Germany than the reverse."

References

Bassi, L., and S. Cheney. 1996. *Restructuring: Results from the 1996 Benchmarking Forum*. Alexandria, Virginia: American Society for Training and Development.

Batt, R., and P. Osterman. 1993. *A National Policy for Workplace Training*. Washington, D.C.: Economic Policy Institute.

Becker, G. 1975. *Human Capital*. Chicago: University of Chicago Press.

Bundesministerium für Bildung und Wissenschaft. 1993–1994. *Grund- und Strukturdaten*. Bonn, Germany.

Colvin, R., and L. Shorgren. 1997. "U.S. 4th Graders Score Strongly in Science and Math." *Los Angeles Times* (June 11), Sec. A1.

Commonwealth of Australia. 1982. *Inquiry into Management Education: Report*. Canberra, Australia, April.

Crouch, C., D. Finegold, and M. Sako. 1999. *Are Skills the Answer? The Political Economy of Skill Creation in the Advanced Industrial Economies*. Oxford: Oxford University Press.

Dore, R. and M. Sako. 1988. *Vocational Education and Training in Japan.* London: Routledge Press.

Finegold, D. 1997. "Developing Global Capabilities." Paper presented at the Center for Effective Organizations Developing Global Capabilities seminar held in Los Angeles, California, April 1.

Finegold, D., and D. Brewer. 1996. "Does Business School Quality Make a Difference? The Impact of Institutional Selectivity on MBAs' Starting Salaries." Working paper, Center for Effective Organizations, University of Southern California.

Finegold, D., and G. Mason. 1996. "National Training Systems and Industrial Performance: U.S.-European Matched-Plant Comparisons." Paper presented at the ILR-Cornell Institute for Labor Market Policies conference "New Empirical Research on Employer Training" held in Ithaca, New York, November 15–17.

Finegold, D., and D. Soskice. 1988. "The Failure of Training in Britain: Analysis and Prescription." *Oxford Review of Economic Policy* 2(2): 22–51.

Finegold, D., and K. Wagner. 1997. "The Search for Flexibility: Workplace Innovation in the German Pump Industry." *The British Journal of Industrial Relations* 36(3): 469–487.

Finegold, D., M. Robbins, L. Galway, C. Stasz, and T. Kaganoff. 1996. *Closing the Knowledge Gap for Transit Maintenance Employees.* Report for the Transportation Cooperative Research Program, RAND, Santa Monica, California.

Finegold, David, Susan Schechter, Jeff Luck, Elan Melamid, Heide Phillips-Shockley, Brent Keltner, Brent Boultinghouse, Frank O'Carroll, Steen Scheuer, and Anne Kathrine Mandrup. 1994. *International Models of Management Development: Lessons for Australia.* RAND, MR-481-IET, Santa Monica, California.

Fuchsberg, Gilbert. 1993. "Harvard Weighs One-Year Version of M.B.A. Program." *Wall Street Journal* (October 29), pp. B1, B6.

Gaugler, Eduard, and Stefan Witz. 1993. *Personalwesen im Europaischen Vergleich: the Price Waterhouse Cranfield Project on International Strategic Human Resource Management.* Universität Mannheim-Lehrstuhl für ABWL, Personalwesen und Arbeitswissenschaft, Mannheim, Germany.

Hall, P. 1986. *Governing the Economy.* Oxford, England: Polity Press.

Haller, Sabine. 1993. "Marktanalyse: MBA-Programme in der Bundesrepublik." Working paper, Fachhochschule für Wirtschaft, Berlin, Germany.

Handy, Charles. 1987. *The Making of Managers: A Report on Management Education, Training and Development in the USA, West Germany, France, Japan, and the UK.* National Economic Development Office, London, England.

Haynes, P. 1991. "A Survey of Management Education." *The Economist* 318: S1–S14 (March 2).

Herrigel, G. 1996. "Crisis in German Decentralized Production." *European Urban and Regional Studies* 3(1): 33–52.

Hollingsworth, J.R., P. Schmitter, and W. Streeck. 1994. *Governing Capitalist Economics*. New York: Oxford University Press.

International Institute for Management Development. 1993. *World Competitiveness Report*. Lausanne, Switzerland.

Kiechel, W. 1994. "A Manager's Career in the New Economy." *Fortune* (April 4): 68–71.

Lawler, E. 1996. *From the Ground Up: Six Principles for Building the New Logic Corporation*. San Francisco: Jossey-Bass.

Lawler, E., S. Mohrman, and G. Ledford. 1995. *Creating High Performance Organizations*. San Francisco: Jossey-Bass.

Lillard, Lee A., and H.W. Tan. 1986. *Private Sector Training: Who Gets It and What Are Its Effects?* RAND, R-3331-DOL/RC, Santa Monica, California.

Lord, M. 1997. "After a Slowdown in the Early '90s, Demand for MBAs is Soaring." *U.S. News & World Report* (March 10): 80–81.

Mason, G. 1996. *Shopfloor Management Skills in Manufacturing: The Formation of Supervisors in the U.S., Germany and Britain*. Report to the U.S. Department of Labor, Washington, D.C.

Mason, G., and D. Finegold. 1997. "Productivity, Machinery and Skills in the U.S. and Western Europe." *National Institute Economic Review* 162(October): 85–97.

National Center for Educational Statistics. 1995. *Vocational Education in the U.S.: The Early 1990s*. NCES 95-024, U.S. Department of Education, Washington, D.C.

OECD. 1993. *Education at a Glance*. Paris: Organisation for Economic Co-operation and Development.

_____. 1994. *The Jobs Study*. Paris: Organisation for Economic Co-operation and Development.

_____. 1996. *Education at a Glance*. Paris: Organisation for Economic Co-operation and Development.

Olson, M. 1971. *The Logic of Collective Action*. Cambridge: Harvard University Press.

Porter, L., and L. McKibbon. 1985. *Management Education and Development*. New York: McGraw Hill.

Reich, R. 1991. "The Real Economy." *Atlantic Monthly* (February): 35–52.

RKW. 1992. *Jahresbericht*. Rationalizierungskommitte der deutschen Wirtschaft, Frankfurt.

Ryan, P., ed. 1991. *International Comparisons of Vocational Education and Training for Intermediate Skills.* London: Falmer Press.

Sabbagh, Karl. 1996. *21st Century Jet: The Making and Marketing of the Boeing 777.* New York: Scribner.

Schneider, Ralf. 1993. "Umfrage zum Stand des MBA in Deutschland" (Parts 1–6). In the *Handelsblatt* Career section, every Friday between October 22/23 and December 24/25, Frankfort.

Scholz, D. 1996. "Neuprofilierung der Weiterbildung zum Industriemeister als Anwort auf neue betriebliche Anforderungen." Berufsbildung in *Wissenschaft und Praxis*, 5.

Snow, Charles C., Scott A. Snell, and Sue Canney Davison. 1996. "Use Transnational Teams to Globalize Your Company." *Organizational Dynamics* 24(Spring): 50–67.

Soskice, D. 1991. "Reconciling Markets and Institutions: An Interpretation of the German Apprenticeship System." Working paper, Wissenschaftszentrum Social Science Research Center, Berlin.

Spreitzer, G., M. McCall, and J. Mahoney. 1997. "The Early Identification of International Executive Potential." *Journal of Applied Psychology* 82(1): 6–29.

Stevens, M. 1996. "Transferable Training and Poaching Externalities." In *Acquiring Skills*, A. Booth and D. Snower, eds. Cambridge: Cambridge University Press.

Streeck, W. 1987. *The Role of the Social Partners in Vocational Training in the Federal Republic of Germany.* Berlin: European Centre for the Development of Professional Training.

_____. 1989. "Skills and the Limits of Neo-Liberalism." *Work, Employment and Society* 3: 90–104.

Weiss, R. 1994. *Die 26-Mrd.-Investition—Kosten und Strukturen betrieblicher Weiterbildung.* Cologne, Germany: Deutscher Institut Verlag.

Wever, K. 1995. *Negotiating Competitiveness: Employment Relations and Organizational Innovation in Germany and the U.S.* Boston: Harvard Business School Press.

4

National Institutional Frameworks and Innovative Industrial Organization

Supplier Relationships in the United States and Germany

Steven Casper
University of Cambridge

This chapter examines how the relationship between the broad institutional configurations of the German and U.S. political economies affects the adaptation, among their firms, of innovative patterns of economic organization. In particular, it examines the transfer of a critical new organizational practice, "just-in-time" (JIT) delivery, from Japan to the U.S. and German economies. Car producers and other large companies have begun outsourcing the production of many sophisticated subassemblies to suppliers under JIT. Despite international markets for capital and goods and services, important differences still exist in institutional frameworks—specifically, in corporate law and industrial relations systems, the two areas most strongly influencing the introduction of JIT delivery strategies. This chapter argues that although JIT delivery has been successfully diffused from Japan to Germany and the United States, differences in national institutional structures have created important differences in the ways that firms in each country support the new system. Furthermore, examining the processes by which JIT delivery has been transferred to the United States and Germany lends insights into the governance of innovation in the two countries.

Innovative forms of economic organization like JIT delivery must be supported by laws and by informal rules negotiated between firms. Together these comprise governance structures that facilitate the flexibility and dynamism created by the new arrangements. At the same time, this organization creates ways to distribute important legal and market risks. JIT delivery is an especially problematic relationship to organize. The delivery of parts directly to final assembly lines that have neither quality-control checks nor large inventories of replacement parts leads to a number of well-known problems. Some defects, particularly nonrandom defects, can halt production and, if not detected before use in assembly, can damage expensive capital equipment or create extensive reworking costs. Because the costs of breakdowns are often large, firms must create both legal entitlements distributing these risks and rules establishing the technical division of labor between companies, in particular, quality-control procedures.

Institutional frameworks influence how companies create the governance structures needed to regulate their relationships. Virtually all studies of the Japanese production system emphasize that JIT delivery emerged as the solution to a unique set of problems and opportunities posed by the structure of Japanese markets and the institutional organization of the Japanese economy (Cusumano 1985). Supplier relationships in the United States and Germany were until recently based on arms-length relationships between large, vertically integrated final assemblers and thousands of small parts suppliers. In Japan, however, final assemblers could not attain such extreme vertical integration. Instead, the *keiretsu* system of cross-ownership within industry groups engendered long-term relationships with key suppliers. Because these suppliers are usually members of the same *keiretsu* industry grouping, final assemblers and suppliers have an incentive to share the legal and market risks entailed in JIT production. As a result, Japanese car manufacturers developed highly collaborative manufacturing relationships with their suppliers. Most of the technical governance problems caused by JIT, such as developing robust quality-control management procedures at supplier companies, were solved through these informal relationships (Sabel 1993).

At least in the short term, institutional frameworks often prevent firms from engaging in innovative forms of organization. How and when can such institutional obstacles be overcome, or, more usefully, reconfigured to help firms introduce modern industrial practices? One solution is convergence. This means that in order for innovative business practices to be transferred across systems, either the relevant market-regulating institutions will have to be changed, or firms wishing to implement new practices will have to opt out of national models and create their own, largely private arrangements. Indeed, some firms in both the United States and Germany have adopted private contracting arrangements between suppliers and final assemblers that mimic key aspects of the Japanese solution, but most have not. Instead, most U.S. and German companies have found alternative governance structures supporting JIT delivery that are compatible with their own institutional environments, which differ substantially from those used by the Japanese. Furthermore, in the German case, the alternatives have been accompanied by a substantial reconfiguration of contracting laws used to demarcate both the legal and technical division of labor between companies in the supplier network. These changes represent a partial reconfiguration (as opposed to a wholesale change) of the German model.

The United States, unlike Germany, has a highly decentralized or "uncoordinated" political economy (Soskice 1999). In general, neither business nor labor has the organizational capacity to develop or enforce collective agreements across labor and/or business organizations. As a result, both the legal system and work organization framework are decentralized and oriented toward private contracting between autonomous agents, in contrast to Germany's "coordinated" business system. In addition to the apprenticeship program and other well-known features of the German industrial relations system, strong business coordination allows the Germans to create a qualitatively different system of legal rules. Under government supervision, important parts of legal frameworks are negotiated between different business associations that represent different corporate interests (manufacturing firms, banks, insurers). This system develops policy instruments that the government can use to regulate how firms distribute legal risks among themselves when setting up supplier network contracts.

More specifically, this chapter makes the following arguments about the transfer of JIT delivery to the United States and Germany. Despite significant problems caused by prevailing supplier relationships in the United States up until the late 1980s, institutional frameworks do not create fundamental hurdles to JIT delivery. While the legal system does not actively promote or transfer the type of arrangements needed for JIT contracting, it does allow firms tremendous latitude in designing their own agreements, which in many cases are successful.   In the area of quality control, patterns of work organization in U.S. plants were actually conducive to developing a new breed of sophisticated quality management systems that facilitate JIT.   Innovation, then, stems from organizations rather than institutions.

In Germany, despite a history of longer-term supplier relationships and, through the apprenticeship system, the existence of skilled workers in most factories, institutional rigidities hinder the introduction of JIT production, at least in the short term.   German legal frameworks actively inhibit the development of the contracts needed to manage the risks created by JIT.   Traditional patterns of work organization are not conducive to the introduction of quality management systems.   Furthermore, gaps in the law have obfuscated what are usually very strict legal regulations that detail how contracting risks are to be spread among firms.   This legal uncertainty has prompted a power struggle between final assemblers and suppliers.   Most final assemblers have pushed responsibility for a number of new legal risks onto suppliers, exacerbating an already difficult transition to JIT delivery.   In these ways, Germany differs strongly from the United States case.

However, in the long term, the German institutional system has a reconfigurative capacity that is lacking in the United States.   Elements of business coordination, exemplified by firms bargaining within trade associations and guided by strong government regulatory oversight, have led to the modification of existing legal frameworks and created new agreements to solve some of the obstacles to JIT delivery.   These agreements have recently been packaged into a new trade association legal framework that is being widely diffused across German industry.   In short, these legal frameworks serve as "blueprints" that firms can use to develop complex industrial organization.   Here again, the German case is quite unlike that in the United States.

The remainder of the chapter elaborates these arguments in detail.   The next section examines JIT delivery in the United States.   This is followed by a section examining the problems created by the German legal framework in adopting JIT delivery and the initial attempts by companies to overcome them.   Then comes an analysis of the broader processes within the German political economy that have reconfigured legal frameworks regulating JIT delivery.   In the conclusion, I summarize the argument and restate the implications of introducing foreign innovations in the two countries.

JIT DELIVERY IN THE UNITED STATES

For decades, U.S. car manufacturers maintained a highly profitable production system, and for this reason, they were slow to see the need for change in automotive technologies during the 1950s and 1960s when manufacturers in Japan and Germany were making advances. An oligopolistic domestic market structure, combined with a lack of serious international competition, allowed final producers to develop very long (five- or six-year) product cycles of basic models and to compete only on the basis of essentially cosmetic annual design changes. Because of the huge size of the U.S. market, large economies of scale could be introduced through mass production with specialized factory equipment. Under these conditions, it made sense for final assemblers to become highly integrated, performing any part of the production process where scale economies could be obtained, which meant that most value-added work took place in-house (Piore and Sabel 1984).

Final assemblers used thousands of suppliers, who produced very simple parts with very little value added. Because these parts were simple to produce, final assemblers routinely kept large inventories of spare parts. Thus, quality was supplied by in-house value-added work, and the price of parts was the main focus of competition among suppliers. Final assemblers typically signed one-year contracts with suppliers. Assemblers usually relied on a number of subcontractors for each outsourced part to ensure fierce competition for contracts. Kenney and Florida (1993, p. 130) quoted a manager of a U.S. supplier company who characterized the traditional system as follows: "The strategy was line 'em up and beat 'em up until you get 'em to a point where they can't make money anymore. Then you've got the best price."

Today, to keep competitive, all car producers in the U.S. marketplace must introduce much shorter (three-year) product cycles, as well as a wealth of new subassemblies based on quickly changing electronics and chemical technologies. Under the old system, U.S. producers kept over 50 percent of the value added in-house. Today they hope to produce no more than 20–30 percent, outsourcing the rest to suppliers who design their own parts and use JIT delivery systems. A number of commentators have pointed out that the traditional U.S. supplier system presented a substantial obstacle to implementing a modern production system (Helper 1991; Womack, Jones, and Roos 1990; Kenney and Florida 1993).

However, recent studies have conclusively shown that a tremendous shift in the organization of U.S. supplier relationships has taken place. Studies conducted between 1992 and 1995 show that the United States has caught up with Japan both in the standard length of contracts offered to suppliers and in the percentage of suppliers using JIT delivery systems (Helper and Sako 1994), and that the United States is actually ahead of Japan in collaborating with suppliers in product development (Ellison, Clark, and Fujimoto 1995; Liker et al. 1996). These results are especially persuasive because similar studies conducted in the late 1980s, often by the same researchers, showed sizable deficits in each of these areas (Helper 1991; Clark and Fujimoto 1991; Womack, Jones, and Roos 1990).

To explain how this transformation was possible, it is necessary first to analyze the traditional system and then investigate the problems that had to be overcome. The old system had two major obstacles to modernizing supplier relationships. First, existing supplier firms were largely unsophisticated, simple parts producers. In the late 1980s, because of the brutality of price competition under the old system, these firms had few resources to invest in the advanced production technology, design capacity, or quality-control procedures needed for more sophisticated production. The first problem in transforming the system was to find sophisticated suppliers or companies capable of becoming "full service." The second problem concerned obstacles to creating effective governance structures to support JIT delivery, as well as obstacles to other parts of new, decentralized supplier networks such as joint product development and long-term price contracts. This problem was exacerbated by the prevailing atmosphere of distrust between suppliers and final assemblers, given decades of ruthless supplier politics. Difficulties in creating effective governance structures were also rooted in the institutional organization of the American political economy.

As to the first obstacle, increased technological sophistication has made it possible for suppliers to produce higher-value-added auto parts. This has spurred a huge entry of sophisticated manufacturing companies into supplier markets.[1]   These new suppliers have the resources to establish wholly dedicated production sites to meet the JIT delivery needs of particular final assemblers. Their individual plants are usually very small. The newest seat production plants of both Johnson Controls and Lear Seating, the largest American JIT seat producers, employ fewer than 45 production workers per shift; but these small production sites are backed up by tremendous corporate resources, including research and development facilities, quality-control and production engineering departments, large financial reserves, and highly trained management teams dedicated to large purchasing, engineering, and sales departments. The nature of the supplier industry has been qualitatively transformed since the late 1980s. The huge size of the U.S. market and direct investment by large foreign suppliers facilitated this transformation. Furthermore, as we will see in more detail, U.S. final assemblers faced virtually no legal obligations to the old supplier base and could easily cut ties.[2]

Understanding the second major obstacle—creating effective governance structures needed to support JIT delivery—is more complex. This requires a systematic examination of the incentives and constraints presented by the broad institutional configuration of the U.S. political economy.

Laws Regulating Interfirm Relationships

In the United States, most sophisticated firms either have their own legal departments or long-standing relationships with large private legal practices. Trade associations play an insignificant role in regulating the contractual dealings of companies. Unlike in Germany, they are for the most part uninvolved in formulating standardized contracts or mediating disputes between companies. While laws and court precedent influence the variety and magnitude of various risks (as in product liability law), they generally do not provide firms with governance structures to regulate their dealings. Legal resources are decentralized among companies and private law firms. As a result of this decentralization of legal resources, the American private sector is in fact highly innovative, but only in providing incentives for firms to create new legal structures facilitating new governance arrangements between companies. There exists no public legal infrastructure to transform innovative private legal arrangements into industry frameworks that can be transferred from firm to firm. Furthermore, the U.S. court system is limited in the type of contracts it can adjudicate because it has no access to private information generated within complex contracting relationships.

U.S. contract law is constructed around classical principles. It assumes that all parties are sophisticated agents; through the enforcement of formal written agreements, it protects their freedom to contract (Macneil 1978). Calls for court reinterpretation of contracts when circumstances have changed, or when the bargaining power between agents is unbalanced, are rare.[3] In adjudicating most breach of contract disputes between firms, U.S. courts usually insist on the fulfillment of even flawed written contracts (Schwartz 1992). Though tort law, especially in the products liability field, provides for large, often punitive sanctions against those responsible for injuring third parties (Priest 1985), contract law does not regulate how contracting parties distribute such liability risks. Parties may contract them out as they see fit. This means that in JIT delivery and other supplier contracts, neither the final assembler nor the supplier has preexisting legal protection against various liability claims.

JIT contracting does not present any fundamentally new legal challenges for U.S. firms. The content of the legally binding part of JIT contracts is settled entirely by the relative bargaining power of the parties involved, on a case-by-case basis. Because final assemblers continue to have tremendous bargaining power over most supplier companies, the legal risks created by JIT are usually borne by suppliers. While JIT delivery creates a dramatic increase in risk exposure to suppliers, from a legal perspective it does not create a dramatically new state of affairs (Bennett 1985); suppliers always have been responsible for damages caused by their defective products. If a defective part is not spotted until after use in assembly, the supplier pays supplementary "rework" costs. If a defective part damages the final assembler's machine tools, the supplier is liable for these damages as well. JIT delivery just increases these risks. It also creates an incentive for suppliers to create and for final assemblers to monitor high-quality control systems.

The Introduction of ISO 9000 Technical Norms

Even with these clear-cut legal rules, there are some risks that cannot be contracted out. Most important are damages to the final assembler's reputation created when defective products reach consumers. It is also difficult to recover all costs from production shutdowns that often occur under JIT delivery when systematic defects are found in outsourced parts. Final assemblers must add informal rules and procedures to the formal contract to manage these extra risks. When large volumes of usually very simple standardized parts were delivered to final assemblers, most defects could be easily spotted by workers and simply replaced through large inventories. Increasingly, defects cannot be easily spotted because they are contained in more complicated components such as brake systems, seats, or preassembled instrument panels assembled by system suppliers with technical know-how that the final assembler does not possess. Furthermore, JIT delivery often makes inspections impossible, either because no spare parts exist or because parts are customized according to flexible logistical systems with very short procurement times (often less than four hours).

Only suppliers' direct monitoring of quality-control procedures can solve these problems. Final assemblers across Japan, Europe, and North America have thus formed relationships with suppliers to monitor their quality control. These agreements vary tremendously, both in style and legal consequences. Japanese-owned manufacturers, both in Japan and in U.S. transplants, rely on informal "hands-on" or collaborative relationships between large quality-management staffs of the final assembler and suppliers (Kenney and Florida 1993). Quality management personnel develop customized quality-control goals with each supplier. They routinely conduct informal audits of each supplier, leading to suggestions for improvements. Repeated visits by assemblers' quality-control staffs, along with the threat that the contract could be terminated, ensure that problems are solved by suppliers (see Sabel 1993 for a more detailed description of this system).

The Japanese transplant producers have successfully introduced collaborative quality-control projects in the United States, both with

Japanese and U.S.-owned supplier companies (Kenney and Florida 1993, pp. 130–145). However, these firms have three advantages. First, they access management know-how from Japan. Second, they do not suffer from negative reputations caused by the mismanagement of supplier relationships that tar American-owned car assemblers. Finally, most Japanese transplant suppliers had preexisting long-term relationships and, in many cases, financial and/or ownership ties with their major customers (Kenney and Florida 1993; Abo 1994). These relationships allowed the Japanese transplants to re-create collaborative quality-control relationships in the United States. When dealing with American-owned suppliers, the Japanese companies have transferred to the United States some of the private institutional arrangements that in Japan facilitate trustful supplier relationships. Toyota, for example, quickly organized supplier associations in an effort to socialize their American-owned suppliers into the Japanese system of organizing supplier relationships (Kenney and Florida 1993, p. 151).

U.S.-owned car manufacturers faced a very different situation. After decades of adversarial "hands-off" relationships, final assemblers lacked both organizational competency (i.e., large quality-control staffs in the purchasing department) and experience in this area. Furthermore, informal quality-control relationships are risky to suppliers. Even though U.S.-owned manufacturers have systematically begun to offer four- to five-year contracts to sophisticated suppliers using JIT delivery, price clauses are still renegotiated yearly. Detailed inspections of the manufacturing process by quality-control experts from the assembler could lead to improved quality control but also expose inside information concerning the company's operating costs. Given a history of opportunistic price politics, suppliers have reason to be risk averse when contemplating collaborative quality-control relationships.

Over time, the big three U.S. car manufacturers might have been able to develop both the organizational competencies and cooperative supplier relationships needed to pursue collaborative quality-control projects. However, they have pursued a different and very interesting course. Sophisticated companies moving into the automobile parts business usually already have quality management systems because they have long been exposed to full legal liability for most damages caused by their products. New companies, or those upgrading from simple parts production to full-service suppliers, have every incentive to introduce such systems. However, from the final assembler's point of view, if JIT delivery is to be used, it is necessary to verify that an airtight quality-control regime exists. In a rare example of extensive cooperation, GM, Ford, and Chrysler jointly developed an ingenious industry framework that not only allows monitoring of each supplier's quality management system without detailed audits by the final assembler, but also provides a blueprint suppliers can use to upgrade or introduce a quality management system. This system was later adopted by the International Standards Organization and became the ISO 9000 set of technical norms.

From a comparative institutional perspective, the development of the ISO 9000 system is extremely interesting, because aspects of U.S. work organization, which in other contexts have proven to be deficient, have actually facilitated the development and diffusion of ISO 9000 norms throughout U.S. manufacturing. Most blue-collar workers in the United States have not been formally trained in industrial skills through an apprenticeship program; instead, they learn on the job. American industrial relations scholars have concluded that a primary reason why a German-style vocational training system has not developed in the United States is the lack of strong employer associations or other coordinating institutions that could jointly develop a curriculum or, more importantly, prevent "free riders" from poaching employees trained by other companies (Soskice 1999; Wever 1995).

When institutional or other constraints hinder the development of one set of competencies within one part of an organization, these competencies must be developed elsewhere if the organization is to survive in a competitive market setting. Most U.S. manufacturing firms have no highly trained workers educated to organize their own work and perform machine maintenance and quality-control duties. As a result, work organization has long been controlled by large middle management staffs of industrial engineers, human resource specialists, technicians, and quality-control experts. Even though many U.S.-owned car manufacturing plants now use extensive job rotation within work groups and train workers in basic machine maintenance and set-up tasks, there is still a broad consensus that the separation of execution and conception that has long characterized American manufacturing plants still exists (Turner 1991). A similar division of work between largely unskilled labor and large specialist middle management staff exists in most sophisticated supplier firms. Hence, most suppliers possess quality-control and other managerial experts who can be used to implement sophisticated quality management schemes.

It is not surprising that broad "scientific management" principles were invented and widely diffused in U.S. firms, because large U.S. corporations were heavily reliant on large middle management staffs to organize all aspects of work (Guillen 1994). These large staffs still exist today and are ideally placed to implement ISO 9000 quality-control norms. Though now diffused worldwide, U.S. car manufacturers were among the first large companies to introduce this system commercially to help alleviate quality-control problems caused by JIT production.

The prototype for the ISO 9000 system was first developed by the U.S. Department of Defense in the 1970s to aid its procurement decisions with commercial contractors. General Motors (GM), as a supplier of jeeps and other military vehicles, had been forced to comply with the military version of the ISO 9000 norm (Casper and Hancké 1999, pp. 964–965). GM worked with Ford and Chrysler to reconfigure the military version of the system into a quality management system suitable for commercial use. By the mid 1980s, the Japanese producers had taken over more than one-third of the U.S. domestic market. GM, Chrysler, and Ford were each attempting to improve quality control at its suppliers in order to introduce both the system supplier strategy and JIT procurement. Facing a common threat and using many of the same local suppliers, the big three could lose little and gain much by cooperating on designing a common quality management system for suppliers.

As this common system now stands, companies meeting different versions of the ISO 9000 norms must incorporate modern quality-control techniques into their assembly operations. The ISO 9000 technical norms are not tailored to particular industries or technologies. Rather, they broadly cover the organization of quality management processes, including design, manufacturing, and packaging and distribution. Procedures examined include statistical process controls, the introduction of quality-control inspections and record keeping within all aspects production, machine maintenance and setup, and the introduction of systematic quality-control meetings and suggestion programs that include production workers, management, and design staff (Paradis and Small 1996). There are different levels of certification, depending on both the type of activities engaged in by the firm and the number of norms actually met (Casper and Hancké 1999).

Widespread use of the ISO 9000 system has prompted the development of certification agencies qualified to conduct ISO 9000–based audits as well as consultants trained to help firms reorganize their quality-control system to meet the norms.

ISO 9000 certification signifies nothing about the excellence or performance of the products of the company being evaluated. These qualities are inherent in the broader design of the product, of which ISO 9000 norms say nothing. But, the norms do ensure that a large number of critical process controls are implemented, which minimizes the probability that defective products will be produced and shipped to the customer. It is particularly important for JIT production that the systematic introduction of statistical process controls virtually eliminates serial defects, which can quickly halt production at the final assembler.

It is not surprising that ISO 9000 norms work well in the context of the U.S. work organization. Workers do not need to be well trained to participate in the system, because in U.S. firms most sophisticated process checks, such as statistical process controls, are performed by specialists. The introduction of documented process checks into most routine work processes also complements job mobility within the firm by increasing job standardization.

The overall result has been a tremendous success. The ISO 9000 norms have helped to rapidly introduce JIT delivery techniques into the U.S. car industry without the accompanying informal quality-control relationships used by the Japanese. In 1991, GM, Ford, and Chrysler again cooperated to modernize the norm series, adding supplementary norms specialized to mass production processes particularly prevalent in the automobile industry.

In sum, incentives provided by the institutional organization of the U.S. political economy combine with the often ingenious strategies of firms to produce a viable new set of supplier network relationships. Facing strong Japanese competition, U.S.-owned car manufacturers rapidly reorganized the composition of their supplier chains and developed and quickly adopted the ISO 9000 technical norms to monitor the quality control of JIT suppliers. While the new strategies were developed by companies, the institutional organization of the political economy facilitated the transformation. The legal system's free-contracting principles acclimated companies to the harsh liability regime introduced by JIT and created few legal obstacles to the rapid change in the supplier base serving final assemblers. The ISO 9000 system allowed the hands-off monitoring needed to overcome a legacy of distrust between U.S. final assemblers and their suppliers. Somewhat paradoxically, ISO 9000 technical norms work so well in the U.S. industrial context because they take advantage of large technical management staffs that are commonly created in U.S. companies because of inadequacies in the vocational training system.

The next section examines the parallel introduction of JIT delivery in Germany. Though the problems facing companies are similar, differences in both the legal and industrial relations systems have necessitated very different strategies by large companies.

JIT DELIVERY IN GERMANY

A large literature describes how "business coordination" facilitates collective solutions within many important domains of German economic life, such as collective wage bargaining, training, and finance (Thelen 1991; Streeck 1984; Wever 1995). Other scholars have pointed out how these frameworks often serve as "para-public institutions" (Katzenstein 1989) linking private economic governance with public regulatory oversight and support of training, research and development, and many other areas of the business system. While there is a large literature connecting the organization of Germany's political economy to its unique patterns of industrial relations, comparatively little analysis has been given to the German legal system. While patterns of work organization are important in Germany, the legal system has been the primary institutional framework influencing the development of governance structures for JIT delivery.

Compared with U.S. law, German law provides a fundamentally different legal context within which firms in supplier relationships must regulate their dealings. In the U.S. case, the legal system was largely benign, neither promoting nor hindering the development of contracting structures suitable for JIT delivery. German companies, on the other hand, faced important legal obstacles when first organizing JIT delivery relationships in the mid 1980s. These obstacles made it difficult for firms to create the necessary legal structures to manage risks. They also combined with incentives produced by the German industrial relations system to hinder the development of adequate quality-control arrangements within supplier firms.

Recently, some German firms have engaged trade associations and other para-public institutions to reconfigure some parts of this legal framework, an ability of the German political economy lacking in the United States. The ultimate aim of this section of the chapter is to explain how and when these agreements emerged. First, however, the section examines the broad character of German legal frameworks regulating supplier networks, how these laws affect companies trying to organize governance structures needed for JIT delivery, and finally, the private, short-term strategies that companies have developed to solve these problems.

Legal Problems Caused by JIT Delivery

Germany's coordinated system of economic governance facilitates the creation of a qualitatively different type of legal environment than exists in the United States. While "good faith" principles have long dominated German commercial law, the broad reorganization of the German economy along "social market" principles after World War II solidified its protective nature. While German law allows large companies extensive freedom to design contracts with other large companies, it strongly regulates contracts between large and small companies. The 1976 passage of the law regulating standardized contracts (AGB-Gesetz) created a broad tool that courts have used to police contracts between large and small companies. Before implementation of the AGB-Gesetz, powerful firms could redesign standard legal entitlements to their advantage and force smaller firms to accept their terms. The AGB-Gesetz provides a legal instrument courts use to control the types of contractual burdens placed on users of preformulated contracts. The general principle of the AGB-Gesetz is that a preformulated clause violates Article 9 of the law when, for economic motives, the contract clause shifts contracting risks in favor of the party writing the contract by inappropriately modifying contract laws set out in standard German civil and commercial law. The most sophisticated supplier chains in the automobile industry still involve dozens, if not hundreds, of firms. As a result, even very complicated long-term contracts regulating relationships with JIT suppliers are often preformulated by the final producer and therefore fall under the scrutiny of the AGB-Gesetz (Grünewald 1995).

Though the technical organization of JIT delivery in Germany is similar to that in the United States, differences in the legal context mean that the same JIT delivery relationships that cause no legal problems in the United States create substantial difficulties in Germany. Articles 377 and 378 of the German commercial code (HGB) contain a nearly 100-year-old law requiring that the (final assembler) undertake a "speedy and thorough" examination of all goods upon delivery. This law limits suppliers' liability when inspections do not take place. In such cases, the final assembler loses all warranty rights and must assume partial responsibility for product liability damages.[4] Because liability cases routinely end in multimillion–deutsche Mark settlements, these legal entitlements are important to the firms involved.

The problem is that the essence of JIT logistical systems is delivery directly to the assembly line for immediate use. Final assemblers argue that the technical organization of JIT precludes them from performing their duties under Articles 377–378 HGB. However, because the "entry inspections" carry with them critical legal entitlements, eliminating them creates a conflict of interest between final assemblers and suppliers concerning the distribution of liability risks associated with defects.

From the final assembler's perspective, if contracts shift the legal responsibility for Article 377–378 HGB inspections to suppliers, substantial liability burdens are also shifted onto suppliers. Final assemblers could demand compensation for both parts and wages incurred in the assembly and the repair of products found faulty due to defects in parts supplied via JIT delivery. Under the old system these defects would be spotted by entry inspections, and legal liability would lie with the assembler. Suppliers would find themselves liable for damages in product liability cases where random defects in parts slip through the production process unnoticed and later cause harm to customers (Grof von Westphalen 1990). Supplier firms turn this logic around. They see no reason why liability risks should be shifted towards them because final assemblers chose to forego historical legal obligations.[5]

Patterns of work organization in small German firms compound the legal problems. Most German workers are highly trained and spend their entire career with one firm. Quality control at most German manufacturing firms is good, but idiosyncratic. Instead of systematized routines developed and implemented by management specialists, skilled workers in German firms usually developed their own quality-control procedures (Schmidt-Salzer 1996; see also Thelen 1991 and Turner 1991 for more on German work organization). Quality-control routines were rarely systematized into formal procedures or supplemented by detailed record keeping. Because the same work groups often survived for decades, informal routines were enough: new recruits could easily learn such procedures from the existing cadre of workers, usually during their three-year apprenticeship. Over the long term, supplier firms could not rely on the strong legal protection from liability damages provided by Articles 377–378 HGB, because their customers could always stop doing business with them if they had continuous quality-control problems; but when introducing new products or work procedures, the law provided short-term protection from quality-control problems.

In the 1960s and 1970s, the German auto parts industry was similar to that in the United States. Most supplier plants produced large quantities of standardized parts. As a result, the work process was fairly simple. Workers were highly skilled, responsible for setting up and maintaining their machines, setting cycle times, and performing quality control according to very effective but often highly idiosyncratic systems. However, in the 1980s and 1990s, as part of the broad switch to the JIT supplier strategy, many supplier firms in the German automobile industry attempted to upgrade their manufacturing processes to win more lucrative contracts for more complicated components or, in some cases, complete subassemblies. For most suppliers, this involved a major redesign of the work process. The new procedures contained more steps. Furthermore, many suppliers had to create flexible manufacturing processes that met different product specifications. This change in processes was an essential part of the JIT strategy.

Because the old informal quality-control procedures often cannot meet the demands of a more complicated work process, suppliers are now more likely to suffer quality-control problems, with their inherent liability problems. But at the same time, most suppliers have been asked to sign a new breed of contract that cedes their traditional Article 377–378 HGB protection against important liability risks.

The Creation of "Quality-Control Agreements" by German Final Assemblers

In the short term, the uncertainty of existing laws has created a void that firms must fill with their own contractual structures. To a certain extent, this creates a bargaining game not unlike that in the United States. Strengthened by their bargaining power over suppliers, final assemblers in the German car industry can create new contracting structures as they see fit. However, they must remain mindful of the likely legal validity of their interpretations should they come under judicial review. Most of these firms use standardized contracting structures, which fall under the purview of the AGB-Gesetz.

When developing JIT delivery contracts, most of the German car manufacturers combined legal clauses with technical agreements regulating quality control. German business practice is for the most part similar to that in the United States in that technical aspects of supplier relationships (such as product specifications or quality-control standards) are normally separated from the formal contract that distributes different legal and market risks. However, faced with the combined problems of developing a more complicated division of technical labor with suppliers and solving the legal uncertainties caused by JIT delivery, the legal departments of most German final assemblers have joined forces with their quality-control experts to create comprehensive "quality-control agreements" (*Qualitätssicherungsvereinbarungen*, henceforward "QCAs").

These agreements usually contain formal abrogations of Article 377–378 HGB inspections, other legal or quasi-legal rules covering warranties and product liability responsibilities, and provisions for settling various problems, such as delay in delivery due to traffic and rework costs. In addition to product specifications, technical provisions contain numerical goals of acceptable error rates and outline the type of quality-control system to be maintained by the supplier. From the late 1980s onwards, most final assemblers adopted the same ISO

9000 norms used in the United States (Casper and Hancké 1999). The final assembler takes responsibility for monitoring whether or not these goals are being met and helps deficient suppliers upgrade their quality-control systems.

While most of the German car producers have set up QCAs containing abrogations of Article 377–378 HGB inspections, important details in their implementation dramatically influence their actual consequences (see Casper 1996 for case studies). The high-end specialist producer BMW, for example, organizes collaborative quality-control relationships that are similar to those of Japanese-owned producers. BMW sends its own auditors to perform supplier certifications, which are supplemented by product technology checks that differ substantially across different types of producers (e.g., textile versus metalworking or electronic technology). Most of the other German car producers pursue more formal quality-control arrangements that look more like those in the United States. Suppliers sign legally binding contracts abrogating Article 377–378 HGB rights allowing "zero defects." They are then supposed to introduce a quality management system specified by the final assembler to achieve these goals. Because the ISO 9000 system is ideal for monitoring quality control across a diverse array of firms, this is the system used by all final assemblers.

German final assemblers have a strong incentive to designate as many firms as possible JIT suppliers and ask them to sign QCAs because it substantially shifts legal risk from their responsibilities. Volkswagen, for example, has recently designated all suppliers making a customized part for VW as JIT. When setting up a new production facility in East Germany, VW explicitly organized its new production site along decentralized production principles. Volkswagen has four JIT suppliers in the area. Deliveries occur several times a day with substantial variation in product specifications. Nine other suppliers deliver complicated but standardized subassemblies on a daily basis. Then there are more than two dozen other local suppliers, most of which make simple stamped parts that are delivered anywhere from daily to weekly. All these firms are officially JIT suppliers that must face the full gauntlet of new legal risks (see Casper 1997 for more on this case).

Because they are an entirely new breed of contract, QCAs have fostered an intense legal debate in Germany. The key issue is whether the Article 377–378 HGB abrogations contained in these documents violate the AGB-Gesetz. Lawyers working for final assemblers argue that they are in effect carrying out Article 377–378 HGB obligations through both stipulating desired quality-control targets and practices to be carried out by suppliers and then monitoring their enactment. Because QCAs substantially improve quality control within supplier firms (to the high levels sufficient for JIT delivery), final assemblers suggest that QCAs make entry inspections superfluous.

Though a number of related court cases point to the interpretation that some QCAs violate the AGB-Gesetz, there has as yet been no specific individual precedent (Casper 1996). This is in part because German parts producers value their long-term supplier relationships more than the possible short-term gains that might be won in a court decision. However, coordinated German supplier companies have other policy instruments at their disposal that American companies lack. Important parts of the industry frameworks governing JIT delivery are being reconfigured to solve some of these problems.

Reconfiguring German Industry Frameworks

"Private lawmaking" has long formed a central part of German associational law. A key difference in the German (relative to Anglo-American) legal system is that in German law, voluntary associations, such as trade associations, have also been allowed to partake in a corporate character and develop strong legal roles and responsibilities (Hueck 1991). Although trade associations in both the United States and Germany have legal departments, those in Germany are much larger and more specialized than those in the United States. In addition to providing services for individual member firms and lobbying the government, trade association lawyers have developed model firm-level contractual agreements. Industry frameworks serve as legal tool kits, helping companies develop the contracting structures needed to set up innovative business dealings. Until recently, these contractual models were usually fairly simple buying or selling agreements (*allgemeine Geschäftsbedingungen*) that small member firms without legal resources could use to set up legally secure business deals. But as the proportion of firms setting up more complicated business ventures has increased, trade association lawyers have attempted to develop more complex model contractual agreements. Though many of these ventures have failed due to lack of consensus among member firms, there have been some successful agreements.

The German Cartel Office is charged with reviewing all proposed industry agreements to assure that agreements break none of Germany's cartel laws. Because of the tightening of German cartel law after World War II, these reviews are very strict. Any trade association agreement whose implementation can foreseeably restrict future competition within a market can be struck down. The principle of voluntarism is at the center of this review, because any model contractual agreement in which participation is binding will be voided. As a result, bargaining within trade associations is usually based on consensus. Where conflicts of interests prevail within a trade association, negotiations will often fail.

The institutional capacity to develop collective solutions to some of the problems posed by JIT delivery is fragile. Even though quality control agreements were first widely used in the German auto industry, conflicts of interest between final assemblers and suppliers have prevented new industry standards from emerging in this sector. Most German car producers oppose the development of a standardized QCA within the Verband deutsche Automobilindustrie (VDA). The hierarchical industrial organization of the automobile sector explains why final assemblers can so easily develop standardized QCA agreements and then present them to suppliers on a take-it-or-leave-it basis.

Instead, an important industry agreement has emerged elsewhere. Though QCAs were initially used most intensely within the auto industry, they have also been employed by companies in other industries with complex supplier relationships. This is particularly true in other advanced technology sectors, such as the machine tool and electronics industries. The trade association representing the electronics industry (ZVEI) has recently developed an important QCA framework that is changing the contours of the JIT delivery debate throughout Germany industry.

Patterns of business coordination are more vibrant in the electronics sector because of its organizational features and the technologies involved. First, most firms are small or medium in size. Relationships with suppliers are typically more balanced because of this greater equality in size. Therefore, individual firms can seldom impose their preferred contractual solution on their supplier partners. Furthermore, the largest two firms in the sector, Bosch and Siemens, are both suppliers and final producers. Their dual role has tempered their willingness to write overtly opportunistic QCAs. Lawyers from Siemens actually played a key role in developing the ZVEI framework.

Technological factors have also played a role. Articles 377–378 HGB only mandate a "feasible" inspection for "visible" damages. Because most electronic parts are microscopic, this limits a feasible-entry inspection. Most firms agree that they should include inspections for obvious physical damages and assurances that products are properly labeled. But because more detailed inspections cannot take place, the supplier must assume liability for other defects. Because of this naturally clear-cut distribution of liability risks and inspection duties, conflict over Article 377–378 HGB inspections is not as great in the electronics sector.

The ZVEI agreement obliges final assemblers to conduct simple Article 377–378 HGB entry inspections, which creates a clear boundary to the risks that must be accepted by suppliers. Entry inspections include checks for transport damages and limited examinations of products to check for visible defects. This modified version of Article 377–378 HGB entry inspection is based on a legal interpretation by ZVEI lawyers, supported by German High Court cases, that final assemblers cannot be expected make entry inspections that demand the development of special expertise or resources (Grünewald 1995). In the electronics industry, the vast majority of errors can only be found through detailed testing of integrated circuits contained in electronic devices. For this technological reason, most supplier firms have adopted detailed quality-control checks into their production processes. Simple spot checks by final assemblers are all that is required to fulfill Article 377–378 HGB obligations. These nominal entry inspections prevent final assemblers from labeling supplier relationships as "just-in-time" purely to serve opportunistic legal strategies that would limit liability through Article 377–378 HGB abrogations.

The agreement also contains supplemental provisions pertaining to the supplier's quality-control system. Like all QCAs, the ZVEI agreement obliges supplier firms to set up a quality management system. However, the precise specifications of this system are determined by the parties to the agreement themselves. ZVEI representatives suggest that most firms will simply use the ISO 9000 norm series most suitable to the technical specification of the supplier's production process, but firms have the option of setting very detailed customized agreements to provide for unique cases.

Overall, the most important attribute of this industry framework is that it creates a reasonable solution to risk distribution issues, through modified exit inspections. Companies using it can direct their energies towards developing the customized supplemental agreements, without fear that these informal parts of their QCA will radically reshuffle contracting risks or break important legal codes. This elasticity shows that it is not only possible to develop complex contracting structures within Germany's associative governance system, but also to structure these agreements so as to place broad limits around the risk distribution issues that often undermine complex contracting relationships.

Furthermore, the ZVEI agreement contains a workable blend of standardized contract terms and supplemental agreement provisions that allow for relationship-specific concerns. The standardized legal terms maintain standard legal entitlements. This brackets off negotiation over many contentious risk distribution issues and assures integration of the agreement with broader German legal codes. Supplementary agreements negotiated by the parties themselves allow some of the relational contracting flexibility that can customize innovative and complex economic relationships.

The ZVEI agreement is one of the most promising examples to date of developing a complex contracting structure within the German associational governance system. Though its review by other trade associations and by the Cartel Office was only completed in January 1995, early signs indicate that it may become widely used within German industry. In the first part of 1995 alone, the ZVEI received over 10,000 requests for copies of the agreement from companies, trade associations, and others. Though there are as yet no statistics on actual usage, interviews suggests that knowledge of the agreement within firms is high, even in non-electronics-related sectors (Casper 1996). For example, the lawyer specializing in contract law within the VDMA, the influential trade association representing the machine tool sector, noted in an interview that the agreement will become a model solution to the Article 377–378 dilemma within German law, stating that it has already been adopted by some machine tool producers.

If the ZVEI agreement is broadly used in the electronics and machine tool industry, it might soon spread to the auto industry as well. This will first happen when powerful suppliers with monopolies on important technologies begin to insist that the ZVEI agreement, or QCAs closely modeled after it, be used in their contract relationships. In the longer term, however, court precedents will play a major role. If, as many German legal scholars predict, the standardized QCA agreements used by most final assemblers are found to violate the AGB-Gesetz, then the ZVEI agreement will begin to look like an increasingly attractive alternative.

CONCLUSION

Innovative organizational practices can be transferred among nations with varying national institutional frameworks. The JIT delivery case shows that, in the face of intense international competition from Japan, companies can engage company organizational structures as well as broader institutional resources existing within their political economies to create new solutions. Companies in Germany and the United States have created viable governance for JIT delivery, but the organization of these governance structures and the way they are regulated within national legal systems differ.

In the United States, the legal system played a passive role and the system of industrial relations, in a somewhat perverse way (because inadequacies of the United States vocational training system were a facilitating factor), provided an ideal setting for the transfer of ISO 9000 quality-control norms from the military procurement system into private industry. In Germany, the highly regulative legal system created important institutional constraints. These constraints were first overcome by the development of quasi-legal quality-control agreements in the auto industry. While the end result in many cases looks similar to the arrangements used in the United States, in Germany these agreements are embedded within an entirely different legal context. In Germany, quality-control norms were formally merged with legal clauses to allow final assemblers to transfer important liability risks to supplier firms. This was facilitated by gaps in the law and by the asymmetrical distribution of bargaining power between final assemblers and suppliers. Industry frameworks are now being developed within trade associations to reregulate JIT delivery within traditional contract law restrictions concerning the distribution of liability risks.

The distinction between "coordinated" and "uncoordinated" political economies allows us to understand key aspects of the these differences. In the United States, the lack of coordinating mechanisms means that industries cannot quickly adapt regulations supporting innovative business organization (for example, trade associations are not in a position to incorporate innovative changes into industry frameworks). Part of the reason why JIT spread quickly in the United States, even without this advantage, was the lack of highly regulative laws. Furthermore, companies had developed considerable private technical and legal resources that allowed them to compete on the basis of innovative governance structures. In this context, it is no surprise that the ISO 9000 norms were reorganized for commercial use in the United States. The drawback is that firms must create their own legal frameworks and cannot gain transaction cost advantages by cooperating within powerful trade associations. Because firms must create their own system of property rights, at least in terms of how contracting risks are managed, the contracting process is often contentious.

The German system allows key aspects of the governance structures used for new patterns of industry organization to become incorporated into public legal frameworks. We have seen how this mitigates some of the risk distribution issues that firms face. Commentators have long noted the importance of the small firm sector in Germany (Acs and Audretsch 1993; Vitols 1995). Germany's regulative system of contract law helps shield small companies from important market and legal risks. This is an important institutional factor influencing patterns of industrial adjustment.

However, highly regulative legal systems are likely to unravel quickly in the face of innovative forms of business organization. This is precisely what happened in the JIT delivery case. In this context, the "reconfigurative capacity" made possible through the system of business coordination becomes a driving feature of the German political economy. Courts and other state actors cannot predict the forms of industrial organization that large companies will adopt or the governance structures they might need to manage complex relationships. However, we have also seen that when the Article 377–378 HGB liability law is applied to JIT delivery contracts, the same large companies lose important legal rights. A fascinating aspect of the German law-making process is that the large companies that are disadvantaged by contract law are simultaneously the pivotal actors in creating and legal-izing new frameworks.

Large German companies create industry frameworks because the governance structures they contain in their organization help socialize the cost of competing internationally and at the same time limit domestic competition over governance structure innovation. Instead of competing privately to create new legal and technical arrangements, many large companies engage trade associations to collectively develop and legalize new legal and technical arrangements for them through the associations' links with the state. So long as the gains from these activities outweigh the costs, large German companies will continue to engage trade associations. However, we have seen that in the auto industry, distributional issues have caused a breakdown in trade associ-ation bargaining. Only in the electronics sector, where differences in industrial organization and technology have created a more favorable setting, has a new trade association been created.

Notes

1. These include large American technology companies such as TRW, which has become one of the largest suppliers of instrument panels; Japanese transplant sup-pliers servicing both Japanese and U.S. final assemblers; former parts divisions from the big three producers, which have been spun off into private companies; and many traditional suppliers that have managed to upgrade their competencies.
2. Though there unfortunately exist no studies of this trend, it seems likely that many of the old parts suppliers were consolidated through mergers and acquisitions into larger firms able to meet the new market conditions.
3. This has led to a major debate within the legal studies field, spurred by the most recent version of the Uniform Commercial Code, which makes "good faith" a central tenet and thus gives ample legal precedent for courts to take a more activist stance if they so choose (Schwartz 1992; Dawson 1983). The most persuasive analyses locate this reluctance to reinterpret the law squarely in the broader frag-mented organization of the U.S. business system.

4. The law states that if the purchaser had properly performed its duties under Articles 377–378 HGB, visible defects would have been found and the future damages avoided (Grünewald 1995).
5. Some legal experts argue that through the incorporation of statistical process controls into inspection systems, final assemblers can still perform entry inspections that satisfy Articles 377–378 HGB while maintaining JIT delivery (Grünewald 1995). Though such checks might decrease the overall efficiency of a firm's JIT logistical system, they would satisfy legal requirements and maintain a traditional allocation of risks between suppliers and final assemblers.

References

Abo, Tetsuo, ed. 1994. *Hybridization of the Japanese Production System in the United States.* Oxford: Oxford University Press.

Acs, Z., and D. Audretsch. 1993. *Small Firms and Entrepreneurship: An East-West Perspective.* Cambridge: Cambridge University Press.

Bennett, R. 1985. "Just-In-Time Purchasing and the Problem of Consequential Damages." *Uniform Commercial Code Law Journal* 26: 322–358.

Casper, S. 1996. "German Industrial Associations and the Diffusion of Innovative Economic Organization: The Case of JIT Contracting." Working paper FS I 96–306, Wissenschaftszentrum Berlin für Sozialforschung (WZB), Berlin, Germany.

———. 1997. "Automobile Supplier Network Organization in East Germany: A Challenge to the German Model of Industrial Organization." *Industry and Innovation* 4(1): 97–113.

Casper, S., and B. Hancké. 1999. "Global Quality Norms within National Production Regimes: ISO 9000 Standards in the French and German Car Industries." *Organization Studies* 20: 961–986.

Clark, K., and T. Fujimoto. 1991. *Product Development Performance: Strategy, Organization and Management of the World Auto Industry.* Boston: Harvard Business School Press.

Cusumano, M. 1985. *The Japanese Automobile Industry: Technology and Management at Nissan and Toyota.* Cambridge: Harvard University Press.

Dawson, J.P. 1983. "Judicial Revision of Frustrated Contracts: Germany." *Boston University Law Review* 63: 1039–1098.

Ellison, J., K. Clark, and T. Fujimoto 1995. "Product, Development, Performance in the Auto Industry: 1990s Update." Working paper no. 95-066, Harvard Business School, Cambridge, Massachusetts.

Grof von Westphalen, F. 1990. "Rechtsprobleme des 'Just-in-Time Delivery.'" *Computer Recht* 9: 567–574

Grünewald, B. 1995. "Just-in-Time-Geschäfte—Qualitätssicherungsvereinbarungen und Rügelast." *Neue Juristische Wochenschrift* 48: 1777–1784.

Guillen, M. 1994. *Models of Management*. Chicago: The University of Chicago Press.

Helper, S. 1991. "How Much Has Really Changed between U.S. Auto Makers and Their Suppliers?" *Sloan Management Review* 32: 15–28.

Helper, S., and M. Sako. 1994. "U.S. and Japanese Supplier Relationships Reconsidered." *Sloan Management Review* 35: 15–28.

Hueck, G. 1991. *Gesellschaftsrecht*. Munich: C.H. Beck.

Katzenstein, P. 1989. "Stability and Change in the Emerging Third Republic." In *Industry and Politics in West Germany*, P. Katzenstein, ed. Ithaca, New York: Cornell University Press.

Kenney, M., and M. Florida. 1993. *Beyond Mass Production*. New York: Oxford University Press.

Liker, J.K., R.R. Kamath, S. Nazli Wasti, and M. Nagamachi. 1996. "Supplier Involvement in Automotive Component Design: Are There Really Large United States–Japan Differences?" *Research Policy* 25: 49–90.

Macneil, I. 1978. "Contracts: Adjustment of Long-Term Economic Relations under Classical, Neoclassical, and Relational Contract Law." *Northwestern University Law Review* 72: 854–905.

Paradis, G., and F. Small. 1996. *Demystifying ISO 9000*. Reading, Pennsylvania: Addison-Wesley.

Piore, M., and C. Sabel. 1984. *The Second Industrial Divide*. New York: Basic Books.

Priest, J. 1985. "The Invention of Enterprise Liability: A Critical History of the Intellectual Foundations of Modern Tort Law." *Journal of Legal Studies* 14: 461–527.

Sabel, C. 1993. "Learning by Motivating." In *Handbook of Economic Sociology*, N. Smelser and R. Swedberg, eds. Princeton, New Jersey: Princeton-Sage.

Schmidt-Salzer, J. 1996. "Öko-Audit und Management-Systeme in organisationsrechtlicher, und versicherungstechnischer Sicht." *Wirtschaftsrechtliche Beratung* 18: 1–10.

Schwartz, A. 1992. "Relational Contracts in the Courts: An Analysis of Incomplete Agreements and Judicial Strategies." *Journal of Legal Studies* 21: 271–318.

Soskice, D. 1999. "Divergent Production Regimes: Coordinated and Uncoordinated Market Economies in the 1980s and 1990s." In *Continuity and*

Change in Contemporary Capitalism, H. Kitschelt, P. Lange, G. Marks, and J. Stephens, eds. Cambridge: Cambridge University Press.

Streeck, W. 1984. *Industrial Relations in West Germany: A Case Study of the Car Industry.* New York: St. Martin's Press.

Thelen, K. 1991. *Union of Parts.* Ithaca, New York: Cornell University Press.

Turner, L. 1991. *Democracy at Work.* Ithaca, New York: Cornell University Press.

Vitols, S. 1995. "German Banks and the Modernization of the Small Firm Sector: Long-Term Finance in Comparative Perspective." Working paper FS I 95–309, Wissenschaftszentrum Berlin für Sozialforschung (WZB), Berlin, Germany.

Wever, K. 1995. *Negotiating Competitiveness: Employment Relations and Organizational Innovation in Germany and the U.S.* Cambridge: Harvard Business School Press.

Womack, J.P., D. Jones, and D. Roos. 1990. *The Machine That Changed the World.* New York: Maxwell MacMillan International.

5
Perils of the High and Low Roads

Employment Relations in
the United States and Germany

Lowell Turner
Cornell University

Kirsten Wever
Rutgers University

Michael Fichter
Freie Universität, Berlin

The German economy today finds itself in a crisis of the "high road"; by contrast, the U.S. economy is experiencing a parallel crisis of the "low road." Although neither of these crises is depression-sized or system-threatening, each is domestically perceived as a serious set of problems that policymakers have yet to solve. Solutions to each set of problems will be guided by understandings of and decisions about the viability of, first, alternative institutional frameworks and, second, different forms of production in the contemporary world economy.

The German high-road crisis is characterized by high unemployment, continuing painful and uneven development in eastern Germany (including east–west conflict within Germany), and new strains between unions and employers and between different employer groups in a formerly stable social partnership. Important actors in both the public and private sector are calling for greatly expanded deregulation and a dismantling of the old social partnership, although employers remain divided on these issues. This crisis has been intensified by international and European competition, internal economic and organizational rigidities, overregulation, high taxes, and certain employers' enchantment with the siren songs of deregulation and the low road to economic growth.

The U.S. crisis is characterized by growing income inequality, a shrinking safety net, and the decline of worker representation. Like the German crisis, it is caused in part by intensified global competition. Unlike in Germany, problems in the United States have also been exacerbated by deregulation, short-term horizons (e.g., quarterly reports to shareholders), and the decline of the labor movement.

Both Germany and the United States, however, have substantial political, economic, and social resources to use in solving their problems. The contemporary crises do not appear for either of these countries to foreshadow a major collapse like that of the Great Depression. We are confident that actors in Germany and the United States can and will pursue reforms, including policy innovations and negotiation. In so doing, we suggest that these societies—the two strongest western economies—have a great deal to learn from each other and from their common experience in the global economy. They do not need, and are unlikely to get, convergence. Yet, each could benefit significantly by adopting elements and aspects of the other's institutions, practices, and policies.

In this chapter, the focus is on employment relations, which we believe are central to the broader economic and social problems in each society. We consider the following two interrelated questions. First, exactly how do the internal and external pressures on employment relations emerge in each country? Second, in what tangible forms do these pressures appear "on the ground," where labor and business (and, more indirectly, other political, social, and economic actors) interact to perpetuate, alter, or scrap certain modes of production, including service delivery, work organization, and negotiation?

At the national level of comparison, the strengths and weaknesses of the German and U.S. models of employment relations are reversed. On the one hand, labor and business in Germany are good at negotiating adjustments to external and internal pressures at the regional, industry, and national levels through extensive and highly articulated institutions of employment relations. On the other hand, with some notable exceptions, the U.S. legal and political system is relatively ill-equipped to coordinate employers and unions in reaching consensual and encompassing strategies for dealing with the economic and associated social pressures of competitiveness.

At the micro- and meso-levels of analysis, comparative strengths and weaknesses are reversed as well. On one hand, U.S. companies and unions have developed deep and far-reaching innovations in organizational structures and processes for labor participation in management and industrial relations more generally (Applebaum and Batt 1994; Rubinstein 1996). Many of these innovations have been dubbed international "best practice" and are even the envy of German employers (Gesamtmetall 1989). On the other hand, at the organizational level, German employers are hampered in developing such innovations by two key factors: first, the functional rigidity and specialization (including management and skill hierarchies) built into most medium-sized and large companies (Finegold and Keltner, in this volume, p. 55) and second, the highly mediated and legally focused function of many (but not all) works councils in codetermination at the workplace (Wever 1995b).

The general challenges facing the two countries parallel this mirrored comparison. Germany's main challenges in the coming years reflect the costs of having taken the high road to competitiveness by preserving high wages and skills, high levels of social security, and relative peace among labor and employer groups while emphasizing diversified quality production (Sorge and Streeck 1988), especially in its powerful export sectors. But the current high unemployment shows that the economic costs of this socially palatable, but in some ways decreasingly competitive, national strategy for growth and social peace have grown substantially, and they are compounded by the continuing high costs of unification. Thus, many German observers, in fact, speak of a crisis of the German model (Streeck 1997a,b).

The chief problems facing the United States, by contrast, arise from the prevalence of companies adopting the low road to competitiveness, with its focus on the reduction of labor costs (whether by downsizing, deunionizing, moving facilities to domestic or foreign nonunion areas, or outsourcing production to nonunion operations). In the advanced capitalist countries, along with low wages come low skill levels, which in turn are increasingly associated with low quality and low productivity. The social inequities that inevitably accompany such a strategy (poverty, wide income disparities) have to date seemed acceptable, at least to the individual companies choosing to take the low road. These growing social problems have, however, become increasingly salient in national and state-level political debates and in the lives of millions of U.S. workers and families.

In the remainder of this chapter, we will briefly compare the basic institutions and practices of employment relations in the two countries, illustrating how in each case these are tightly embedded in broader political economic structures, such as financial systems, the organization (or disorganization) of the employer community, labor law, and the nature of government intervention in employment relations. This is followed by a comparison of the past strengths and emerging weaknesses of the high- and low-road approaches and a discussion of how the problems associated with each path are exacerbated by and reflected in the structures and strategies of employment and industrial relations. We then illustrate this argument in concrete empirical terms by considering how unions, works councils, companies, employer associations, and governments at various levels are in fact dealing with their respective challenges. Here, we clarify the extent to which variation in actor strategies can be found even within the two countries. Finally, we conclude with a discussion of the implications of our findings and an argument for what German and U.S. business, labor, and government actors and policymakers can learn from each other as they try to sort out the unfamiliar problems they face.

EMPLOYMENT RELATIONS COMPARED

Germany

The key strength of German employment relations is their inclusiveness, which manifests itself in a bias toward negotiating change between multiple interested stakeholders (Turner 1998; Soskice 1990; Thelen 1991; Wever and Allen 1993; Keim and Unger 1986). Government and the labor and employer communities can all be credited with upholding critical aspects of the negotiated postwar German model of organized modern capitalism.[1] The government provides a strong and stable institutional infrastructure: framework conditions (*Rahmenbedingungen*) within which business and labor have found incentives to engage in a collaborative relationship from the micro- to the macrolevel (Allen 1989). The business community takes full advantage of the stability offered by a partnership-oriented labor movement and the supportive framework offered by the social market economy, prominently including a highly skilled workforce. Sure and steady management practices harness worker and manager skills that are based on functional specialties and that favor concrete technical skills over general managerial qualifications (Berg 1993). The unions actively try to influence technological change by promoting high levels of productivity and skill development (Turner 1991). German unions, for their part, have been prepared to modify their wage demands when the overall economic good seems to call for such a position. They have allowed the works councils (which are formally independent, enterprise-based, and legally mandated) to negotiate the terms of changes in human resource policies to fit the needs of specific companies (Wever 1994). This dynamic remained essentially in place in unified Germany in the 1990s (Turner 1998).

More specifically, employment relations in Germany involve several interconnected levels of negotiation. Collective bargaining contracts are bargained at the level of the region and industry (e.g., between the North Rhine–Westphalian branches of the chemicals industry union, Industriegewerkschaft Chemie [IG Chemie], and the industry's employer association). In most sectors, patterns are established in certain regions roughly coinciding with the German states (*Länder*), which are then adopted in other regions. In some cases, individual company agreements set patterns as well: for instance, Volkswagen negotiates directly with the metalworkers union IG Metall. These bargains cover employers in a range of companies. As such, the agreements are perforce highly general, laying out wage, hour, and working condition minima.

These minima are the legal contractual bases used as starting points for further negotiations at individual companies, typically between a personnel or human resource department and the works council. However, even within companies, different interpretations and permutations of the collective bargaining agreement may be negotiated: the company works council may reach one set of broad agreements, while works councils at various production or service delivery locations may have more refined agreements as well. In many cases, the individual works councils may agree on wages that exceed the minima established by the collective bargaining agreements. In short, the works councils effectively translate loose-framework collective bargaining agreements into company- or workplace-specific practices of labor–management relations.

Formally independent of the unions, the councils represent about two-thirds to three-quarters of German workers and are most prevalent in larger companies. These work councils are in constant contact with representatives of personnel or human resources departments, jointly implement the collective bargaining agreement, and participate closely in most basic personnel decisions. The councils have veto power over hiring, firing, transfers, and overtime decisions, among others, and must be consulted regarding most other personnel-related matters. German managers credit the existence of the councils—that is, management's ability to negotiate directly with a company- or workplace-specific body of worker representation—for much of the country's vaunted postwar labor peace (Wever 1995b).

On the subject of labor peace, it is important to note that different unions approach negotiations with employer associations differently (Markovits 1986). In general, the unions representing metalworkers, public employees and employees in the media sector have been regarded as fairly forceful and confrontational. However, these unions—particularly the huge IG Metall—have made the most progress in addressing workers' interests, for instance, on the issue of a shortened work week. IG Metall has also been the most strategically adept and forward thinking of the German unions, in part because of its tremendous resources. The union normally associated with the most cooperative tact is IG Chemie, representing workers in the chemicals industry.[2] Because of the unions' close relationships with the works councils, a given union's approach to management usually, but not always, reflects that of the works councils within that union's industry. Thus, for example, works councils in the chemicals sector tend to be fairly quiescent and seldom take the initiative to make organizational change within the firm. By contrast, councils in the metalworking industry are frequently involved in, and sometimes the initiators of, significant work reorganization.

The overall labor–management relationship in Germany is a constructive and cooperative one. In addition to the reasons suggested in the previous paragraph, this cooperation can be attributed to the fact that significant dispute resolution procedures take place outside the workplace. Disputes are adjudicated by a separate system of labor courts, peopled by representatives of labor, business, and government, which is widely regarded as fair and effective.

Suddenly, however, beginning with the breathtaking events that started with the symbolic fall of the Berlin Wall in 1989 and resulted in German unification less than a year later, a great deal of uncertainty, a host of unfamiliar challenges, a vast economic burden, and an entirely new political landscape have been inserted into German employment relations, and politics more generally. Germans must now deal simultaneously with the new terms of economic and political competition that have been introduced by unification; the supplanting of traditional forms of production organization; the high cost of German labor; the weak international position of the German high-technology sector; and the pressures for Germany to conform to the less "social" market standards of other European Union (EU) countries and of the rest of the world (Streeck 1997b; Streeck and Vitols 1994). The German employer community—increasingly focused on labor costs—has asserted growing unease about the continued viability of further investments. Germans refer to this problem in shorthand as the *Standort Deutschland* (Germany as a production site) debate.

In short, the stability, labor peace, "export miracle," and other characteristics of the postwar German political economy have been undermined by the pressures of foreign competition, the high cost of unification, and the need to cut social spending to meet EU standards for Economic and Monetary Union. Under these circumstances, in the eyes of employers and of the current Schröder government, the negotiated high-road (high wages, high skill development, high social standards) strategy has become too costly. One important manifestation of German employers' dissatisfaction with the status quo is their falling rate of membership in sectoral employer associations, which negotiate collective bargains with industry unions. Nonmembership in an employer association means a company is not bound to the terms of the industry bargain, allowing the company to lower its labor costs. Because the centralized foundation of German employment relations has long been considered a key to its postwar socioeconomic success, the weakening of these institutions is clearly cause for concern to labor (Silvia 1997).

Two other significant challenges threaten traditional German employment relations. First, institutional, organizational, and strategic rigidities limit the substance of what can be negotiated among the major actors, especially in comparison to "best practice" cases in the United States. German managers have been deeply but, in comparative terms, narrowly trained for functionally specialized deployment (Lane 1989; Maurice, Sellier, and Silvestre 1986). Thus, German management faces peculiar problems in developing the cross-functionality and flexible new forms of organization that are necessary to compete in the contemporary international marketplace (see also Finegold and Keltner in this volume, p. 55).

The second challenge in adopting less rigid forms of work and production organization lies in the structure and functions of the works councils as laid out by the Works Constitution Act of 1952 (as amended). The councils exist as a buffer between workers and personnel or human resource management departments. They seldom conduct substantive negotiations with operations managers or workplace-level supervisors; needless to say, in most cases, neither do frontline workers. Most of the councils' functions concern managing human resources, not enhancing labor participation in decision making at the point of production.

The United States

The key strength of U.S. employment relations is the relative weakness of institutional constraints on the parties involved. This freedom makes possible world-class innovations in work and production organization, training initiatives, service delivery mechanisms, teamwork, and cross-functional collaboration, as well as a capacity for organizational innovation of all kinds.

As in Germany, the government has created an institutional framework to govern employment relations. That framework consists of two main pieces: first, the National Labor Relations Act (commonly known as the Wagner Act), the Railway Labor Act, and parallel public sector legislation, which govern union–management relations and union structure in the unionized sector of the economy; and second, the proliferation of laws governing individual employee rights (regarding, for instance, Equal Employment Opportunity [EEO] and affirmative action). These rights are cumbersome for the employer because they can end in lawsuits and significant financial penalties and because they can be filed by either individual employees or groups of employees. Nevertheless, most medium-sized and large companies are benignly inclined toward EEO and affirmative action. In contrast, U.S. employers have historically objected ardently to collective employee and union rights as codified in the Wagner Act and other legislation.

Today, the rules of union organizing, union recognition, collective bargaining, contract administration (grievance procedures), strikes, and lockouts—which were established by the New Deal framework (centering on the Wagner Act)—are hotly contested by many employers (Babson 1995). Many, perhaps most, U.S. firms are run by managers who believe that unionization necessarily entails significant increases in labor costs without any balancing improvements in company competitiveness such as the higher levels of productivity and quality that have been shown in Germany (Milkman 1997). Moreover, like much of the public at large, many managers associate U.S. unions with contentious and combative labor relations, long and bitter strikes, and a hostile work climate. Unions' legislative efforts to make it illegal for companies to hire permanent replacement workers in case of a strike have been bitterly and successfully fought by the employer community and their conservative (Democratic as well as Republican) allies in Congress. Indeed, even the extremely mild labor law reform that was introduced in 1978 under the Democratic Administration of Jimmy Carter, to ease the rules connected with organizing new workers, failed to pass into law.

Outside the legislative arena, companies have used multiple legal and illegal means to prevent their employees from unionizing. Many companies with some union operations have shifted production toward nonunion operations, often in more conservative regions of the country, where states' right-to-work laws constrain union rights. Union decertification campaigns have grown in number and have been increasingly successful since the early 1980s. Partly as a result, union density (the percentage of the workforce that is unionized) has dropped from almost 25 percent in the late 1970s to less than 14 percent currently. This drop has occurred despite continuing relative union gains in the public sector. Private sector unionism has dropped to less than 10 percent.

The U.S. union movement has been under constant and effective attack by these forces for more than two decades, which is one important reason why unions are often unwilling to engage in cooperative endeavors with employers. The overall weakness of organized labor in the United States is not the only impediment to joint labor–management innovations. Another important factor is the law itself. The Wagner Act lays out in detailed terms precisely how unions can organize, what issues they may bargain over, and what sorts of structures must attach to any joint labor–management efforts. Thus, for example, many impressive examples of union initiatives in organizing and labor–management innovations, strictly speaking, may violate U.S. labor law.[3]

Unlike in Germany, collective bargaining in the United States is conducted for the most part at the company level (often supplemented by plant-level agreements). Variation across union contracts is great, and contracts are in general lengthy, highly specific, and arduous to negotiate. Although some of the more powerful unions in some ways resemble German-style industry unions, there are many examples of conflict among unions over the right to represent particular groups of workers.[4] Given the diversity of U.S. negotiation strategies, the existence of over a hundred different unions (craft and industrial unions as well as some hybrids), and the lack of coordination among employers in standardizing employment relations (bargaining minima or maxima), the United States cannot benefit from the channels of communication and bargaining alternatives that are available to German unions, works councils, and employers.

Having no "second channel" of worker representation (such as the works council), unions in the United States typically have no influence over the kinds of human resource management decisions that require the input of works councils in Germany and most other advanced industrial countries. In most cases, therefore, the adage that "management acts, the union reacts" continues to hold true. In addition to strategic considerations based on widespread management hostility toward unions, this lack of a second channel is another way in which U.S. unions are discouraged from taking an active role in labor–management or organizational innovations. Moreover, lacking a separate forum for dispute resolution (such as the German Labor Courts), the tensions accompanying labor disputes are played out in the same arena in which contracts are negotiated and administered. This combination introduces a potentially hostile mood and distributive considerations into the very forum in which joint labor–management endeavors could hypothetically be developed. Given this combative institutional and cultural landscape, it is no wonder that strike rates are much higher in the United States than in Germany.

Under these circumstances, it is noteworthy—if not astonishing— that in some cases that are discussed in the following section, unions, workers, and managers have jointly developed highly refined methods for changing the nature of labor–management relations and the organization of work and production. In part, their ability to buck the trend rests on the fact that while the government's intervention in labor relations is detailed and intensive on paper, it is relatively minimal in fact. Examples of labor–management participation and cooperation leading to significant organizational and relational innovations have seldom been challenged legally.

Successful U.S. cases of the transformation of traditional labor– management relations (Kochan, Katz, and McKersie 1986) can partly be attributed to the lack of organizational and strategic rigidities that in Germany limit the substance of what can be negotiated. Even the German-based operations of many U.S.-owned companies appear to be characterized by the kinds of cross-functional, flexible new forms of employment relations and work and production organization that are necessary to competitiveness in the contemporary international marketplace but so difficult to engender in the German context (Wever 1995a).

Finally, U.S. innovations are in some ways aided by the lack of German-style works councils: where joint innovations are negotiated and implemented, unions and workers typically negotiate intensively and regularly with operations managers and production supervisors, rather than being limited to formal relations with the personnel or human resources function. Rather than acting as a buffer between workers and management in these cases, unions act as facilitators in ongoing negotiations with management about how work is best accomplished.

In short, the employment relations systems and environments of the United States and Germany are strikingly different, each with its peculiar strengths and weaknesses. The strengths of the U.S. system, at the level of organizational innovation, are mirrored in reverse by the weaknesses of the German system, while German strengths in institutional supports for extensive dialogue and negotiations between labor and management are the reverse image of the great tensions between the parties in U.S. labor relations.

A COMPARISON

How can these problems in U.S. and German employment relations systems be categorized, and what are the implications of the comparison? After several decades of pursuing the unilateral managerial (United States) and negotiated (German) paths, each country now faces a path-specific set of problems.

The German high road entails what Streeck (1992) has dubbed a "virtuous circle," in which the production of high labor-value-added, high-quality goods, requiring a skilled and cooperative core workforce, promotes exports. These qualities in turn have reinforced the "diversified quality production mode," relying on broad, long-term consensus among the social partners. This is the sort of consensus that has historically led German unions to forfeit wage gains in times of recession, in the knowledge that they would be recouped in boom times.

The U.S. low road, by contrast, entails efforts to substitute technology for labor, to cut labor costs where possible, with the inevitable resistance and—given employers' power in the United States—eventual weakening of organized labor. Another low-road strategy is to move operations to geographical locations (foreign or domestic) where labor costs are lower by virtue of the weakness of or lack of unions or low prevailing wages. Relatively high labor costs and the need to produce high labor-value-added goods and services persist in many industries (e.g., high-tech services, some areas of high-tech manufacturing, and most business services). But in the United States, even in industries in which a high road is possible (e.g., in telecommunications, where service quality is critical to productivity and profits), we see firms not only pursuing the high road (e.g., BellSouth, at least until 1994) but also building a lower labor cost, nonunion model without labor participation in management and with less concern for skill development (Batt and Darbishire, in this volume, p. 17).

Germany

In Germany, as suggested in the previous section, institutions and the traditions they have spawned are necessarily associated with slow, thorough, widely negotiated, and usually more or less consensual change. The notoriously slow pace of organizational decision making is lamented by German managers, as are Germany's high labor costs. The problem is that to speed change would require the relaxation of regulations, which in turn would require significant adjustments to the current institutional framework of employment relations. Such adjustments would lead (indeed, have led) to noticeable increases in social unrest. Public sector strikes in the 1990s in Germany surrounding the government's efforts to cut the social wage attest to this. For employers, simply to move in the direction of the low road, even with the tacit support of powerful forces in the federal government, would be to court levels of social strife (e.g., conflicts, strikes, slowdowns, or sickouts) which might require the sacrifice of both labor peace and the high level of overall skills.

Germany's endangered position on the high road both influences and is influenced by German employment relations. The effect on labor relations is perhaps more obvious. Employers and their associations have been calling for lower labor costs for at least 20 years. To the extent that employers choose not to join or to drop out of employer associations, it is usually because they wish to avoid the terms and conditions of sectoral contracts.

But the structure of employment relations also contributes to the problem. To the extent that unions are unwilling to allow more substantive issues to be negotiated at the local level between individual companies and works councils, employers will continue to find at least some public and political support for their efforts to lessen the influence of the collective representatives of employees.

It should be noted that IG Metall and IG Chemie, as well as several other unions, are on the record as being willing to renegotiate the structure of collective bargaining and the relationship between industry-wide and company-specific issues and dynamics. Indeed, IG Metall publicized proposals on this topic as early as 1990 (IG Metall 1990). Nevertheless, the positions of the unions and the employer associations remain distant from each other, especially in the pattern-setting metal industries. In part, this is because the unions are, not surprisingly, loath to give up too much centralized control over the terms and conditions of employment. The rift between labor and management can also be attributed in part to some employers' near-total embrace of the United States' more unilateral approach to labor–management relations, which reduces labor's participatory powers far more than the unions, most works councils, or German society as a whole accept.

Many employers try to create worker participation and worker–management cooperation programs that bypass the councils and the unions, with mixed success. Again, this tactic resembles the more uni-lateral managerial approach associated with employment relations in the United States. In this regard, given the need for strong labor repre-sentatives in order to preserve the noted benefits of the German system, such methods exemplify how the structure of employment relations not only contributes to, but also clearly reflects, Germany's high-road problem.

The United States

In the United States too, the employment relations system—along with other features of the institutional landscape, such as employer organization (Casper, in this volume, p. 93)—helps create the problem as well as being directly affected by it. The contentious nature of union–management relations in most of the unionized sectors makes it reasonable for many employers to try to weaken unions or seek non-union settings in which to produce their goods and services. The so-called "union wage premium"—the wage benefit enjoyed by union workers as compared with workers in similar jobs who are not union-ized (currently between 25 and 30 percent of wages)—is also part of the problem from the standpoint of employers.[5] Union work rules his-torically have hampered employers in their efforts to deploy workers efficiently. For instance, craft workers maintain narrow jurisdictional lines, meaning that a plumber on site may be prohibited by the labor contract from changing a light bulb if electricians are otherwise occupied or not available. This is another reason why many employers dread unions.

The U.S. employment relations system also lacks institutional structures that offer employees pride in their negotiation skills and in implementing workplace transformation initiatives. Ever since the rise of the industrial unions in the 1930s, the emphasis of many unions has been more on the organization of existing workforces, skilled and unskilled. The skills of those workers and the improvement of their skills have seemed less important to the unions than simply consolidating the labor movement sufficiently to gain significant bargaining power vis-à-vis individual employers. To the extent that skill development has played an important role, programs have been fostered and often delivered primarily by craft unions, which have strong interests in preserving their jurisdictional lines (in competition with other unions) and maintaining control over the content of skills (e.g., hampering efforts to broaden skills in line with more flexible work practices). There is much to applaud in the revitalization of the labor movement that followed the 1995 election of a dynamic labor leader, John Sweeney, to the presidency of the American Federation of Labor–Congress of Industrial Organizations (AFL-CIO). Sweeney has reorganized the federation and hired an intelligent, young, and dynamic new top staff. Nevertheless, the main priorities of the new AFL-CIO are similar to those of the industrial unions in the 1930s, which focused more on organizing new members than on improving and protecting skills. Moreover, union density declined again in the year 2000, and organizing efforts are waning in many unions.

Employment relations also takes its toll on the U.S. institutional landscape. Most obviously, employers' sustained attack on the labor movement (including decertifications and the legal and widespread practice of firing pro-union employees) has created a climate in which any union cooperation with management is by itself a remarkable accomplishment. Moreover, because a union can be decertified or a plant's operations moved to a nonunion setting or even abroad, most joint labor–management programs exist *de facto* at the sufferance of management. There are in fact numerous cases in which employers have suddenly and/or arbitrarily terminated apparently successful and far-reaching participatory experiments.[6]

Another important way in which the U.S. institutional framework contributes to the low-road problem stems from the pressures created by its financial system. Most U.S. companies view stockholders as their primary stakeholders. Stockholders and lenders require quarterly statements of profits and losses. Many managers' salaries are tied to financial performance on a quarterly basis. This system creates a host of incentives to develop short-term business strategies. However, investments in human capital, to say nothing of investments in efforts to transform the labor–management relationship, offer only long-term returns. Moreover, since they are in many regards qualitative, these "returns" are hard to measure. In many cases, it cannot be shown quantitatively that productivity or quality improvements follow from these kinds of investments. Many managers could argue, in fact, that such improvements would have occurred even in the absence of training or labor–management participation programs.

What, then, would indicate that significant inroads into solving the low-road crisis were being made? We argue that at the very least, significant changes to current U.S. labor law would be needed. In addition, changes to the financial system and to other features of the institutional landscape (such as antitrust laws, which limit extensive employer coordination of the sort that is possible in Germany) could improve the situation.

The high- and low-road crises of Germany and the United States can be understood in terms of the mirrored reversals that we explained earlier: the U.S. context is better suited to promoting organizational innovation and change (albeit usually without the involvement of collective worker representation), while the German context better coordinates the main actors, such that change is negotiated and consensual (albeit slow).

ALTERNATIVE STRATEGIES FOR REFORM

In this section, we examine the main priorities and current action plans of the parties on the ground in both countries, focusing on how they might be helping to solve the problems we have covered in this chapter.

Germany: Renegotiating the Negotiated System

In contrast to that in the United States, employment in Germany is characterized by high and relatively egalitarian average wages and partnership relations in firms and workplaces that largely reflect a high-road philosophy (Streeck 1997b). The question of how to create alternative strategies for reform from those available to labor and management is central to the future of the Germany's well-structured, integrated, and interdependent socioeconomic system. The debate over which strategies to use raises the question of whether all or at least some basic elements of the system should be reformed or whether single, company-oriented proposals should be advanced. Discussions among the various sectors of the economy and within unions and employer organizations have produced conflicting opinions on how to best solve these problems.

The two key problems concern the instrument of comprehensive sectoral collective agreements and the role of works councils and co-determination. Sectoral collective agreements set wage minima and define the spectrum of company-level bargaining over work organization. Critics regard this system as too inflexible and cumbersome to function effectively. Indeed, the highly structured character of the German system and the overall strength of the unions and the employer associations have been maintained despite membership losses on both sides and numerous steps toward decentralization. Many negotiated agreements are moving toward more decentralization, including, for instance, recommendations by the sectoral bargaining agents for company-level negotiations on a variety of topics (Bahnmüller and Bispinck 1995, p. 157). The breadth of topics that can be negotiated at the company level has grown, especially in regard to the flexibility of working hours. For example, in 1994, the employer association Gesamtmetall and IG Metall signed a contract allowing management and works councils to negotiate agreements that reduce working hours even though these hours may deviate from the general provisions of the sectoral contract.

It is still common practice for employer associations and trade unions to reach pragmatic compromises that exemplify the negotiated workings of the system. Nevertheless, the employer associations have been uneasy with the centralized system and have offered proposals for revamping it. Probably the most widespread of these is the demand for including "opening clauses" (*Öffnungsklauseln*) in sectoral agreements. These clauses explicitly empower management to bargain with their works councils over the replacement, modification, or extension of sectoral contract provisions (Gesamtmetall 1996). Some form of "opening clause" is now included in many contracts. The chemical industry employer association was among the first to negotiate opening clauses with IG Chemie in reaction to "intensified international pressure on costs" (BAVC 1996).

Over the past few years, all members of the union federation (Deutscher Gewerkschaftsbund [DGB]) have proposed revisions to the coordinated bargaining system. Although many unions are still wary of employer reform ambitions, the door to reaching a negotiated reform remains open. Sectoral and regional contracts negotiated by IG Metall and Gesamtmetall for 1997–1998, for instance, call the sectoral collective agreement "a sound instrument, open to the future, for regulating industrial relations . . . offering . . . sufficient room for tailored solutions to specific company problems" (Hüsson 1997, p. 5). Most union leaders recognize the need to make revisions that reflect the enormous structural changes in the economy. Membership drops in the employer associations support this view because unions depend on employer associations as representative bargaining partners.

The position of the DGB unions is reflected in a policy statement passed at an extraordinary congress of the DGB in November 1996. Seeing the need to "recognize the differentiated interests of employees" and contribute to "shaping the different realities of individual branches and enterprises," the unions called for the introduction of "packaged options" into the sectoral contract (Deutscher Gewerkschaftsbund 1996, p. 14). For example, in the chemical industry, the social partners have made a point of promoting company-level agreements that are embedded in the structures of sectoral collective bargaining (Terbrack 1997, p. 7). Agreements reached in 1996–1997 in the metalworking and electrical industries provide standard options for regulating the relationship between bonus pay and absenteeism (Arbeitsstelle Nationale und Internationale Gewerkschaftspolitik 1997).

The unions remain basically opposed to relinquishing their negotiating rights to company or workplace agents. Not only do they shy away from potentially chaotic conditions, which could be the result of blanket deregulation, but they also fear for their own organizational stability. Although the German unions have fared well in comparison with many unions in other industrialized countries, they too have been plagued by organizational problems and membership flight (Fichter 1997). Employer associations suffer from many of the same problems. Mid-sized and small enterprises especially have become highly critical of the wage negotiation policies of their associations, calling for more resistance to union demands. In many instances, dissatisfaction has grown to the point that withdrawing from employer associations has become an increasingly popular strategic alternative, and newly established enterprises are refraining from joining at all. This conflict of interests is particularly evident in the large Gesamtmetall,[7] but is of no less concern to a number of other associations, for example, those in the pharmaceutical industry (Schnabel 1995, p. 59).

The burden on local management and works councils to find company-specific solutions to the complex issues of jobless growth and employment insecurity has grown. Works councils are under pressure to assent to extensive cuts, which sometimes break from binding sectoral contracts (as is often tacitly acknowledged by employer associations) to avoid membership losses. Below the level of contract stipulations we find, as Streeck (1996, p. 91) noted, "coalitions between employers, who want to lower their wage and possibly their training costs, and employees, who prefer lower pay to no pay at all."

Efforts by the unions to stem this tide and combat rising unemployment have been unsuccessful. In January 1994, IG Chemie signed a two-year contract allowing firms to hire new workers at 95 percent of the contract rate for the first year of employment. However, if a person is hired who has been unemployed for 6 months or for at least 12 months within a 24-month period prior to being hired, then pay would be at 90 percent of contract wages for the first year. Such employees would have only "temporary" status. Similar plans exist in eastern Germany, where special government regulations forced the unions into such agreements. IG Chemie decided on its own to pursue this path in western Germany, hoping to create employment. However, recent surveys suggest this has not happened. The union is now negotiating with the employer association over the introduction of lower pay rates in selected segments of the chemical industry such as plastics and synthetic fibers.

In late 1995, Klaus Zwickel, head of IG Metall, presented a three-year plan called an "Alliance for Jobs" (*Bündnis für Arbeit*), in which the union offered to forgo real wage increases if employers would agree to create 300,000 new jobs. This was an attempt to build on the Volkswagen model, a highly respected 1994 agreement that saved some 30,000 jobs by reducing the average number of weekly hours to 27.5 (Hartz 1994; Volkswagen AG and IG Metall 1994). The Kohl government tried to get substantive tripartite negotiations started on the basis of Zwickel's proposal. The employer associations ultimately demurred on the grounds that the prerogative for job creation lay with individual employers. Instead, they proposed company-level job alliances. These, however, turned into something quite different from what IG Metall intended (Zeuner 1996): rather than giving up pay increases to create new jobs, works councils found themselves negotiating pay cuts (within the limits of sectoral contracts) to secure existing employment and prevent further dismissals (Rosdücher and Stehle 1996, p. 325). A full-scale national Alliance for Jobs would have to wait for the election of a Red-Green government in 1998. Although already an important forum, tripartite Alliance negotiations remain difficult and often quite adversarial.

Codetermination and works councils have contributed to establishing a climate of negotiation and compromise that has long had a positive effect on the stability and adjustment capacity of the German economy (Bacon, Blyton, and Morris 1996). In the past decade, however, the scope and complexity of issues bargained at the enterprise level have increased tremendously. Even those who champion the instruments of workplace negotiations wonder how these negotiations can deal with the problems of job loss, outsourcing, and the increasing mobility of capital and labor (Dieterich 1997, p. 3). Creating new patterns of work organization and introducing concepts of group and individual responsibility raises new issues that the existing channels of employer, worker, and union representation must learn to handle (Müller-Jentsch and Sperling 1995, p. 42; see also Baethge and Wolf 1995, p. 243).

Employment relations in eastern Germany since 1990 can be understood largely as a battle on the part of German unions and large employers to defend the high road for unified Germany. Unions and employer associations from the west moved into the collapsing east beginning in 1990 to establish comprehensive collective bargaining. When employers backed down on their wage parity commitment in 1993, eastern workers, led by IG Metall, waged an extraordinarily successful strike to defend rising wages along the high road (Turner 1998).

Management-led innovations in the east have also furthered high-road potential for unified Germany. Western managers, for example, soon discovered that modern forms of shop-floor and office teamwork could be introduced on the basis of socialist brigade legacies more easily and with less resistance than in the established west. Eastern plants, such as VW in Mosel and Opel in Eisenach, have become pattern setters, not only for modernization in the east but also for work reorganization in the west.

Finally, the European Union (EU) contains a variety of systems of employment relations. Analysts argue about whether the weakness of Europe-wide social regulations may lead to the eventual dismantling of the existing structures of codetermination and works councils (cf. Streeck 1997b; Turner 1998).

The United States: Isolated High-Road Struggles in a Low-Road Context

Employment relations in the United States are characterized above all by numerous approaches and relationships, both traditional and innovative. The traditional approach, as influenced by the concept of "scientific management," viewed employees to a large extent as replaceable parts that could perform as directed. As an outcome, the assembly line revolutionized production in the United States, and factory-developed approaches to personnel management spread widely throughout the economy in both the private and public sectors. In reaction, in the 1930s, industrial unions grew and engaged in damage control, establishing rules and workplace rights and improving wages and benefits. Although there were exceptions as well as considerable variation, employee relations in the twentieth century to a large extent continue to be largely adversarial.

In spite of many famous cases of innovation and countless quality and employee involvement programs, the U.S. workplace remains significantly hierarchical and authoritarian (Babson 1995; Milkman 1997). Adversarialism is more muted in nonunion workplaces, although the decline of the labor movement has opened up a representation gap by removing the possibility of a meaningful, independent voice in the workplace for many employees (Freeman and Rogers 1995).

Nonetheless, both successful and failed innovation has been widespread since the 1970s as changing world markets have highlighted the value of active employee participation. In notable cases, unionized workplaces have been transformed from conditions of "armed truce" to showplaces of employee participation and labor–management collaboration. The auto industry, for example (the traditional model in adversarial labor–management relations), has set new standards of excellence and provided new patterns for emulation. In 1984, an old, highly adversarial General Motors (GM) plant in California reopened as NUMMI (New United Motor Manufacturing Incorporated, a GM–Toyota joint venture), demonstrating a reformed management approach oriented toward shop-floor teamwork and active union participation in decision-making processes. These changes showed the potential for transforming the U.S. workplace, with its experienced workforce, into a more productive and less conflictual environment (Brown and Reich 1989; Turner 1991). NUMMI provided Toyota's now-famous "lean production" model, which quickly succeeded in proving the value of a new team structure with enhanced training and input from employees. The dark side of lean production also became clear at NUMMI, as employees complained about intense production pressure and only very narrow participation opportunities—such as brainstorming how to bring a 60-second work cycle down to 58 seconds (Turner 1991; Babson 1995).

The highly successful Saturn experiment in Tennessee took United Autoworkers–General Motors (UAW–GM) collaboration several steps further (Rubinstein 1996). Like NUMMI, this case is widely known and intensively studied, and certain lessons stand out in sharp relief. First, profound change is possible within the loose framework of employment relations in the United States. Second, close company–union collaboration from the very start can foster quality-enhancing information flows, consensual decision making, and active participation and commitment all around. Third, extensive labor participation can lead directly to pathbreaking innovation in production organization, from design through sales and service. However, the failure of the

Saturn model to spread to other settings reflects continuing organizational inertia at both GM and UAW and continuing ambivalence about making high-road investments in a low-road economy (Wever, Batt, and Rubinstein 1996).

Beyond the auto industry, there are numerous other successful cases of labor–management partnership at unionized workplaces. These include AT&T, NYNEX, BellSouth, Xerox, Corning, United Airlines, and others. Two recent examples in very different industries offer tantalizing models for future agreements elsewhere. Levi-Strauss and UNITE (the apparel and textile workers union) agreed in the early 1990s to a broad framework agreement that incorporated union officials into decision-making processes throughout the organization. It pledged the company not to oppose union organizing campaigns at nonunion Levi-Strauss plants. Kaiser Permanente (a large, HMO-oriented healthcare and hospital organization), after extensive negotiations with its 14 unions, agreed in 1997 to a similar deal. This agreement included a provision applying to Kaiser's 30,000 nonunion employees (out of a total workforce of 80,000). The company agreed to recognize a new union as soon as 51 percent of eligible employees at a given Kaiser workplace signed cards indicating their desire to unionize. This breakthrough (known as card-check recognition) eliminated the need for the bitter election campaigns that are usually necessary to create a union in a nonunion workplace and that, win or lose, so often leave an enduring legacy of hostility and adversarial relations. Each of these cases can be understood in part as an attempt by companies and unions to shift from a low-road to a high-road orientation.

Numerous innovations in employment relations also exist at nonunion workplaces, many of which serve explicitly or implicitly to keep unions out. In the auto industry, so-called Japanese transplants (Toyota in Kentucky, Nissan in Tennessee, and Honda in Ohio) run high-productivity, lean-production operations similar to NUMMI but without union representation. Motorola and Hewlett-Packard are widely cited examples of nonunion high-road approaches that emphasize good working conditions, decent pay and benefits (relative to comparable pay in a given geographical area), mechanisms for limited employee voice, and a strong focus on skill development and employee training.

More common in nonunion workplaces is the low road. This reflects an enduring tradition, dating back to the beginnings of industrialization, of authoritarian management that is focused on controlling workers and holding down wages. These, of course, are the very circumstances in which unions emerged as workers' champions in the 1930s, but the long decline of the U.S. labor movement has permitted the continuation and expansion of this hierarchical and/or paternalistic trend. Examples range from apparel sweatshops in New York City to poultry processing plants across the South and Japanese-owned manufacturing plants, with the auto assembly plants standing out as rare exceptions to the low-road approach (Milkman 1995). Even as firms modernize their production organizations both domestically and through cross-national networks, low-road problems of labor sweating and income inequality continue to persist and in many cases intensify (Harrison 1994).

Low-road production persists in the United States largely because there are so few obstacles or disincentives to low-road practices (such as low wages and benefits, intensified pressure on the workforce, and minimal skills development). Positive incentives for high-road investment, such as adequate government support and regional labor–management partnerships for vocational training, are rare. These are the incentives one finds in Germany and in pathbreaking U.S. cases such as the Wisconsin Regional Training Partnership (Parker 1997).

The current revival of the U.S. labor movement could encourage more labor–management partnerships and is the most hopeful sign of a possible solution to the U.S. low-road crisis. New labor leaders and activists at the AFL–CIO, as well as at some of its member unions, are pouring increased resources into organizing campaigns and developing innovative strategies to reach low-wage workers. In the meantime, some unions are encouraging labor–management partnerships at individual companies and in regional skills programs as part of a proposed broad union–employer "social compact" (Greenhouse 1996). Although this current revival is in its infancy and may or may not succeed in the long run, the prospects appear more hopeful than at any time over the past 20 years (Turner, Katz, and Hurd 2001). The experience of numerous high-road countries in northern Europe demonstrates that, in the interest of economy-wide domestic or export-oriented high-road production, it is essential to close off low-road options. One obvious way to do this is through comprehensive collective bargaining coverage.

In sum, the United States can boast important high-road innovations and partnerships at particular companies and in certain areas. Yet
such innovations continue to occur within a low-road context. Because
employers in the United States are relatively unconstrained and face
broad choices in strategic planning, they can make high-road choices
while simultaneously continuing on the path of least resistance toward
new or continuing low-road production strategies. Serious income
polarization and a generally weak skills base (Reich 1991; Harrison
1994) suggest that the low road occupies an all-too-large, if not a pre-
dominant, position in the U.S. economy. Incentives necessary to promote the high road include expanded government participation and
legislation; employer and labor support, including joint efforts to promote skills training; and more labor–management partnerships like
those at Saturn, Levi-Strauss, and Kaiser-Permanente, as well as the
continued expansion of union organizing efforts.

CONCLUSION: IMPLICATIONS FOR
MUTUAL LEARNING

What can the United States and Germany learn from each other
regarding necessary reforms to contemporary employment relations in
each country? Because their institutional contexts are so different, we
do not believe that employment relations in these two countries will
converge. But we do believe that the key actors, including policymakers in each country, have much to learn from the experiences of the
other.

It is clear that German employers, as well as unions, feel increasingly intense pressure to decentralize the coordinated sectoral and
regional bargaining system that has been credited with much of their
post-war economic miracle. Perhaps the most important lesson for
German unions, works councils, and employers and employer associations is the old saying, "Don't throw the baby out with the bath water."
The baby represents what still works well in the German system,
including the institutional mechanisms that can help negotiate successful methods for addressing new and unfamiliar economic pressures

(international pressures as well as those stemming from unification and membership in the EU).

Most Germans are aware of the most extreme dangers of U.S.-style "cowboy capitalism" such as the low-road problems we have explored in this chapter. If significant deregulation and decentralization are initiated, the unions and employer associations would be enfeebled and might end up with more U.S.-style problems, including significant social problems (from poverty and crime to the rise of neo-Naziism). One would hope that the unions remain strong enough and retain enough overall social legitimacy that they could prevent such developments from going too far. Germany cannot afford to take a path which might result in social turmoil or in undermining the negotiating climate which characterizes the German political economy; either would be an economically costly outcome.

A second important lesson for Germany is that truly flexible workplace innovation can be compatible with high-road institutional structures. As noted above, the low-road context, within which stunning organizational innovations occur even in unionized settings, is far from supportive of high-road innovations. It is, in fact, an impediment. The low-road context of U.S. industry has isolated the Saturn innovations and now threatens to undermine completely BellSouth's labor–management innovations (see Batt and Darbishire, in this volume, p. 17). In fact, if a larger portion of the U.S. economy were characterized by high-road practices (union coverage, high wages, skills development, and proactive labor–management partnership), locally developed innovations would likely be easier to implement and transfer to other settings.

However, this is not to say that there are no features of the German system of employment relations that might impede such innovations. On the contrary, as noted earlier, possible impediments to innovation can be found in the formal nature of relations between works councils and personnel or human resource departments, in the relatively rare occurrence of direct worker participation in decision making at the point of production (see also Wever 1995b), and in the functionally specialized and rigid aspects of organizational structures and management strategies (see Finegold and Keltner, in this volume, p. 55). In other words, to emulate U.S.-style innovations, Germans would need to

retain and restructure appropriate institutional supports without cling-
ing to institutional constraints associated with the German model.

U.S. policymakers and practitioners can learn from Germany's
experience that the benefits of an economy-wide high-road approach
cannot be achieved in a totally independent, company-by-company
employment relations setting. To move toward a higher road in the
United States, employers must create forums for collective information
sharing, standard setting, and possibly even resource pooling. The
Wisconsin Regional Training Partnership, mentioned earlier, represents
a rare example of regional efforts in this direction (Parker 1997; Parker
and Rogers 2001). Similar, less developed efforts in this direction are
under way in the states of California, New Jersey, and Washington.
These regional development projects illustrate that institutions can be
created to support mutually beneficial outcomes without entailing
unacceptable institutional constraints on individual employers or
unions.

This lesson is reinforced by the fact that Germany's efforts at imi-
tating low-road practices—in the rare cases where this has been possible—are not working. For instance, employer-based agreements in the
chemicals sector for trading off job creation against wage or hour concessions have often resulted in wage concessions in exchange for mere
employment security, not job creation.

Finally, it can hardly be a coincidence that growing domestic,
social, and economic problems in the United States coincide with the
erosion of the national skills base. As unions have lost power, wages
and benefits have stagnated, and skills have followed closely behind.
Absent the capacity of governments, companies, or employees to pay
for skills development, educational and training institutions have not
been able to slow the low-road descent. Low-road jobs have swelled
the ranks of the "working poor," who must now compete with former
welfare recipients in transition from welfare to low-paying jobs. This
inevitably will continue to lead to increased homelessness, ill health
(absent national health care), and other social problems. As these problems mount, employers will be less and less interested in hiring from
this large segment of the workforce. As the flight of capital from urban
centers illustrates, employers may relocate because there is too much
cheap labor available (while their businesses depend on skilled or

highly skilled labor), just as easily as they may do so because there is too little.

In short, Germany cannot solve high-road problems with low-road practices; in the United States, labor and management are confronting the problems of trying to take the high road in a low-road context. Solutions for the two countries are necessarily different, but they can be unified in a common conceptual framework. Actors must differentiate between the constraining and supportive aspects of coordinating institutional frameworks. Centralized forums for setting standards, sharing information, and pooling resources are important components of a successful high-road strategy. However, rigid, functionally specialized and hierarchically organized approaches to innovation and change entail unnecessary institutional constraints. The Germans have a surfeit of both coordinating institutions and organizational rigidities; they need to maximize the former and minimize the latter. Political economic actors in the United States must for the most part build high-road institutions and practices from scratch (using Germany and other countries as guides) while avoiding hierarchical rigidities and constraints. Can this be done? Not without a great deal of U.S.-style innovation and experimentation. Such innovation is currently revitalizing the U.S. labor movement; there is no reason why it cannot also be channeled into high-road institution building.

Notes

1. The German "negotiated" and the U.S. "unilateral" approach to competitiveness are defined in Wever (1995b). They refer to the institutional structures that engender negotiations about organizational change between labor and management in Germany and that discourage such negotiation, creating incentives for a more unilateral managerial approach, in the United States.
2. In October 1997, IG Chemie merged with the miners and leatherworkers unions, forming IG Chemie-Bergbau-Energie.
3. Two examples will illustrate this problem. The Service Employees International Union's Justice for Janitors campaign organizes workers in an entire labor market rather than in the legally prescribed company-by-company fashion. The internationally acclaimed Saturn experiment, designed by General Motors and the United Autoworkers union to include full-fledged union participation in all areas

of management, is inconsistent with the law's stipulation that union members cannot perform managerial work and with its provisions for choosing union representatives.

4. For example, disputes between the International Brotherhood of Teamsters and the International Association of Machinists and Aerospace Workers date back several decades.

5. It is important in this connection to note that some research suggests that the union wage premium is more than compensated for by increases in unionized employers' productivity, which can be attributed to the fact that unions can spur employers to seek more effective ways of organizing work and production and to the fact that productivity and quality-enhancing participatory programs involving unions, workers, and managers may be more successful and long lasting in unionized settings than in nonunion companies (Freeman and Medoff 1984; Applebaum and Batt 1994; Kelley and Harrison 1992).

6. The most famous of these cases is that of Eastern Airlines in the mid 1980s. A more recent and still unfolding case is that of BellSouth, whose Excellence Through Quality programs, designed together with the Communication Workers of America, became in the late 1990s a lower priority for a management team struggling to come to terms with increasingly heavy competition resulting from the final phases of telecommunications deregulation. In this connection, the telecommunications industry is an interesting German–United States comparative case study, because in Germany the union has been far more successful in defending the rights of workers in the wake of deregulation (Batt and Darbishire, in this volume, p. 17).

7. The case of IBM leaving Gesamtmetall was more the result of the employment profile and market dynamics in the computer industry.

References

Allen, Christopher S. 1989. "Regional Governments and Economic Policies in West Germany: The 'Meso' Politics of Industrial Adjustment." *Publius* 19(4): 147–164.

Applebaum, Eileen, and Rosemary Batt. 1994. *The New American Workplace: Transforming Work Systems in the United States*. Ithaca, New York: ILR Press, Cornell University.

Arbeitsstelle Nationale und Internationale Gewerkschaftspolitik. 1997. "Verhandlungsergebnis für die Beschäftigten der Metall- und Elektroindustrie in Berlin und Brandenburg, Tarifgebiet I." 1997. In *Gewerkschaften und Industrielle Beziehungen*, GA/NF47/01, Politische Wissenschaft, Freie Universität, Berlin, January.

Babson, Steve, ed. 1995. *Lean Work: Empowerment and Exploitation in the Global Auto Industry*. Detroit: Wayne State University Press.

Bacon, Nicolas, Paul Blyton, and Jonathan Morris. 1996. "Among the Ashes: Trade Union Strategies in the UK and German Steel Industries." *British Journal of Industrial Relations* 34(1): 25–50.

Baethge, Martin, and Harald Wolf. 1995. "Continuity and Change in the 'German Model' of Industrial Relations." In *Employment Relations in a Changing World Economy*, Richard Locke, Thomas Kochan, and Michael Piore, eds. Cambridge: MIT Press, pp. 231–262.

Bahnmüller, Reinhard, and Reinhard Bispinck. 1995. "Vom Vorzeige- zum Auslaufmodell? Das deutsche Tarifsystem zwischen kollektiver Regulierung, betrieblicher Flexibilisierung und individuellen Interessen." In *Tarifpolitik der Zukunft: Was wird aus dem Flächentarifvertrag?*, Reinhard Bispinck, ed. Hamburg, Germany: VSA-Verlag, pp. 137–172.

BAVC. 1996. *Presse-Information: Rheingauer Erklärung*. Bundesarbeitgeberverband Chemie, October 18, p. 2.

Berg, Peter. 1993. *The Restructuring of Work and the Role of Training: A Comparative Analysis of the United States and German Automobile Industries*. Ph.D. dissertation, Department of Economics, University of Notre Dame, Notre Dame, Indiana.

Brown, Claire, and Michael Reich. 1989. "When Does Union–Management Cooperation Work? A Look at NUMMI and GM–Van Nuys." *California Management Review* 31(4): 26–44.

Dieterich, Thomas. 1997. "Mitbestimmung im Umbruch." *Arbeit und Recht* 45(1): 1–13.

Deutscher Gewerkschaftsbund. 1996. *Die Zukunft gestalten. Grundsatzprogramm des Deutschen Gewerkschaftsbundes*. DGB National Board, National Congress in Dresden, Germany, November 13–16.

Fichter, Michael. 1997. "Trade Union Members: A Vanishing Species in Post-Unification Germany?" *German Studies Review* 20(1): 83.

Freeman, Richard B., and James L. Medoff. 1984. *What Do Unions Do?* New York: Basic Books.

Freeman, Richard B., and Joel Rogers. 1995. "Workplace Representation and Participation Survey: First Report and Findings." Unpublished document, Department of Economics, Harvard University, Cambridge, Massachusetts.

Gesamtmetall. 1989. *Mensch und Arbeit: Gemeinsame Interessen von mitarbeitern and Unternehmen in einer sich wandelten Arbeitswelt, Gesamtverband der metallindustriellen Arbeitgeberverbände*. Cologne, Germany.

_____. 1996. *Reformprojekt Flächentarif*. Freiburg, Germany.

Greenhouse, Steven. 1996. "Union Leader Urges Companies to Forge Alliance with Labor." *The New York Times*, October 27, p. 23.

Harrison, Bennett. 1994. *Lean and Mean: The Changing Landscape of Corporate Power in the Age of Flexibility*. New York: Basic Books.

Hartz, Peter. 1994. *Jeder Arbeitsplatz hat ein Gesicht: Die Volkswagenlösung*. Frankfurt, Germany: Campus Verlag.

Hüsson, Norbert. 1997. "Die Qual der Wahl." *Die Quelle* 48(1): 5.

IG Metall. 1990. *Tarifreform 2,000: Ein Gestaltungsrahmen für die Industriearbeit der Zukunft*. Frankfurt, Germany.

Keim, Rüdiger, and Hans Unger. 1986. *Kooperation statt Konfrontation: Vertrauensvolle Zusammenarbeit zwischen Arbeitgeber und Betriebsrat*. Cologne, Germany: Informedia.

Kelley, Mary Ellen, and Bennett Harrison. 1992. "Unions, Technology and Labor–Management Cooperation." In *Unions and Economic Competitiveness*, Larry Mishel and Paula Voos, eds. New York: M.E. Sharpe.

Kochan, Thomas, Harry Katz, and Robert McKersie. 1986. *The Transformation of American Industrial Relations*. New York: Basic Books.

Lane, Christel. 1989. "Industrial Change in Europe: The Pursuit of Flexible Specialization in Britain and West Germany." *Work, Employment and Society* 2(2): 141–168.

Markovits, Andrei. 1986. *The Politics of West German Trade Unions*. New York: Cambridge University Press.

Maurice, Marc, Francois Sellier, and Jean-Jacques Silvestre. 1986. *The Social Foundations of Industrial Power: A Comparison of France and Germany*. Cambridge: MIT Press.

Milkman, Ruth. 1995. "The Impact of Foreign Investment on U.S. Industrial Relation: The Case of California's Japanese-Owned Plants." In *The Workers of Nations: Industrial Relations in a Global Economy*, Sanford M. Jacoby, ed. New York: Oxford University Press, pp. 127–154.

_____. 1997. *Farewell to the Factory: Auto Workers in the Late Twentieth Century*. Berkeley: University of California Press.

Müller-Jentsch, Walther, and Hans Joachim Sperling. 1995. "New Technology and Employee Involvement in Banking: A Comparative View of British, German and Swedish Banks." In *Organized Industrial Relations in Europe: What Future?* Colin Crouch and Franz Traxler, eds. Avebury, England: Aldershot, pp. 229–248.

Parker, Eric. 1997. *Regional Industrial Revitalization: Implications for Workforce Development Policy*. Working paper no. 114, Center for Urban Policy Research, Rutgers University, New Brunswick, New Jersey.

Parker, Eric, and Joel Rogers. 2001. "Building the High Road in Metro Areas: Sectoral Training and Employment Projects." In *Rekindling the Movement: Labor's Quest for Relevance in the Twenty-First Century*. Lowell Turner, Harry G. Katz, and Richard W. Hurd, eds. Ithaca, New York: IRL Press, Cornell University.

Reich, Robert. 1991. *The Work of Nations*. New York: Alfred A. Knopf.

Rosdücher, Jörg, and Oliver Stehle. 1996. "Concession Bargaining in the USA and Employment Creation Politics in Germany," *Industrielle Beziehungen, Zeitschrift für Arbeit, Organisation und Management* 3(4): 10.

Rubinstein, Saul. 1996. *Rethinking Labor and Management: Saturn and the UAW; The Governance and Supervision of High Performance Team–Based Work Systems.* Ph.D. dissertation, Massachusetts Institute of Technology, Sloan School of Management.

Schnabel, Claus. 1995. "Entwicklungstendenzen der Arbeitsbeziehungen in der Bundesrepublik Deutschland seit Beginn der achtziger Jahre: Eine Analyse unter besonderer Berücksichtigung der Arbeitgeberseite." In *Sozialpartnerschaft und Arbeitsbeziehungen in Europa*, Michael Mesch, ed. Vienna, Austria: Mane, pp. 53–74.

Silvia, Stephen. 1997. "Political Adaptation to Growing Labor Market Segmentation." In *Negotiating the New Germany*, Lowell Turner, ed. Ithaca, New York: Cornell University Press.

Sorge, Arndt, and Wolfgang Streeck. 1988. "Industrial Relations and Technical Change: The Case for an Extended Perspective." In *New Technology and Industrial Relations*, Richard Hyman and Wolfgang Streeck, eds. London: Basil Blackwell.

Soskice, David. 1990. "Reinterpreting Corporatism and Explaining Unemployment: Coordinated and Non-Coordinated Market Economies." In *Labor Relations and Economic Performance*, Renato Bunetta and Carlo Dell'Arigna, eds. Proceedings of the Conference of the International Economic Association held in Venice, Italy. Vol. 95. Houndsville, United Kingdom: MacMillan, pp. 170–211.

Streeck, Wolfgang. 1992. *Social Institutions and Economic Performance: Studies of Industrial Relations in Advanced Capitalist Economies.* London: Sage Publications.

_____. 1996. "Anmerkungen zum Flächentarif und seiner Krise." *Gewerkschaftliche Monatshefte* 47(2): 86–97.

_____. 1997a. "Der europäische Sozialstaat der Nachkriegszeit ist endgültig passé." *Frankfurter Rundschau*, January 6.

_____. 1997b. "German Capitalism: Does It Exist? Can It Survive?" *New Political Economy* 2(2): 237–256.

Streeck, Wolfgang, and Sigurt Vitols. 1994. "European Works Councils: Between Statutory and Voluntary Adoption." In *Works Councils: Consultation, Representation, Cooperation*, Joel Rogers and Wolfgang Streeck, eds. Chicago: University of Chicago Press and the National Bureau of Economic Research.

Terbrack, Hans. 1997. "Reform durch Verknüpfung." *Die Quelle* 48(1): 7.

Thelen, Kathleen. 1991. *Union of Parts: Labor Politics in Postwar Germany.* Ithaca, New York: Cornell University Press.

Turner, Lowell. 1991. *Democracy at Work: Changing World Markets and the Future of Labor Unions.* Ithaca, New York: Cornell University Press.

_____. 1998. *Fighting for Partnership: Labor and Politics in Unified Germany.* Ithaca, New York: Cornell University Press.

Turner, Lowell, Harry Katz, and Richard Hurd, eds. 2001. *Rekindling the Movement: Labor's Quest for Relevance in the Twenty-First Century.* Ithaca, New York: ILR Press, Cornell University.

Volkswagen AG and IG Metall. 1994. "Bezirksleitung Hannover, VW-Tarifvertrag." *Arbeit und Recht* 42(6): 230–232.

Wever, Kirsten S. 1994. "Learning from Works Councils: Five Unspectacular Cases from Germany." *Industrial Relations* 33(4): 467–481.

_____. 1995a. "Human Resource Management and Organizational Strategies in German- and U.S.-owned Companies." *International Journal of Human Resource Management* 6(3): 606–625.

_____. 1995b. *Negotiating Competitiveness: Employment Relations and Organizational Innovation in Germany and the United States.* Boston: Harvard Business School Press.

Wever, Kirsten S., and Christopher S. Allen. 1993. "Financial Systems and Corporate Governance in Germany: Institutions and the Diffusion of Innovations in Comparative Context." *Journal of Public Policy* 13(2): 183–202.

Wever, Kirsten S., Rosemary Batt, and Saul Rubinstein. 1996. "Innovation in Isolation: Labour-Management Partnerships in the United States." *The Economic and Labour Relations Review* 7(1): 67–87.

Zeuner, Bodo. 1996. "Von der 'Konzertierten Aktion' zum 'Bündnis für Arbeit'?" *Frankfurter Rundschau*, November 13.

The Authors

Rosemary Batt is an assistant professor of human resource studies at the Industrial and Labor Relations School, Cornell University. She is co-author of *The New American Workplace: Transforming Work Systems in the United States* (Cornell University Press, 1994).

Stephen Casper is a university lecturer at the Judge Institute of Management Studies, University of Cambridge. His current research investigates the diffusion of entrepreneurial business models in Europe.

Owen Darbishire is a university lecturer in management studies at the Saïd Business School, University of Oxford, and is also a fellow of Pembroke College.

Michael Fichter is a lecturer in the Department of Political Science and executive director of the Center for Labor Relations at the Free University of Berlin.

David Finegold is an associate research professor at the Marshall School of Business, University of Southern California.

Brent Keltner is CEO and co-founder of English Exchange, Inc., an e-learning company targeting the English Language Training market in Asia. He was previously a consultant to Citigroup's Global Technology Strategy group and a researcher at the RAND Corporation.

Lowell Turner is a professor of international and comparative labor, School of Industrial and Labor Relations, Cornell University.

Kirsten Wever is an assistant professor of labor studies and employment relations in the School of Management and Labor Relations, Rutgers University.

Cited Author Index

The italic letters *f*, *n*, and *t* following a page number indicate that the cited name is within a figure, note, or table, respectively, on that page.

Subject Index

The italic letters *f*, *n*, and *t* following a page number indicate that the subject information is within a figure, note, or table, respectively, on that page.

About the Institute

The W.E. Upjohn Institute for Employment Research is a nonprofit research organization devoted to finding and promoting solutions to employment-related problems at the national, state, and local levels. It is an activity of the W.E. Upjohn Unemployment Trustee Corporation, which was established in 1932 to administer a fund set aside by the late Dr. W.E. Upjohn, founder of The Upjohn Company, to seek ways to counteract the loss of employment income during economic downturns.

The Institute is funded largely by income from the W.E. Upjohn Unemployment Trust, supplemented by outside grants, contracts, and sales of publications. Activities of the Institute comprise the following elements: 1) a research program conducted by a resident staff of professional social scientists; 2) a competitive grant program, which expands and complements the internal research program by providing financial support to researchers outside the Institute; 3) a publications program, which provides the major vehicle for disseminating the research of staff and grantees, as well as other selected works in the field; and 4) an Employment Management Services division, which manages most of the publicly funded employment and training programs in the local area.

The broad objectives of the Institute's research, grant, and publication programs are to 1) promote scholarship and experimentation on issues of public and private employment and unemployment policy, and 2) make knowledge and scholarship relevant and useful to policymakers in their pursuit of solutions to employment and unemployment problems.

Current areas of concentration for these programs include causes, consequences, and measures to alleviate unemployment; social insurance and income maintenance programs; compensation; workforce quality; work arrangements; family labor issues; labor-management relations; and regional economic development and local labor markets.